George F Clarke

Double Entry Bookkeeping for Technical Classes and Schools

George F Clarke

Double Entry Bookkeeping for Technical Classes and Schools

ISBN/EAN: 9783744644464

Printed in Europe, USA, Canada, Australia, Japan

Cover: Foto ©Andreas Hilbeck / pixelio.de

More available books at **www.hansebooks.com**

Double Entry Bookkeeping

FOR

TECHNICAL CLASSES AND SCHOOLS

BY

GEORGE F. CLARKE,

Associate of the Society of Accountants and Auditors (Incorporated 1885)

(BY EXAMINATION).

LECTURER ON BOOKKEEPING AND ADVANCED ACCOUNTS AT THE ST. HELENS
MUNICIPAL TECHNICAL SCHOOL, &C., &C.

———

ADAPTED FOR THE BOOKKEEPING EXAMINATIONS OF THE UNION OF LANCASHIRE
AND CHESHIRE INSTITUTES, SOCIETY OF ARTS, CIVIL SERVICE,
COLLEGE OF PRECEPTORS, &C.

———

LONDON :

GEE & CO., PRINTERS AND PUBLISHERS, 34 MOORGATE STREET, E.C.

—

1898

PREFACE.

A S a teacher of the important subject which is set forth in this book, I have found some difficulty in obtaining a suitable text-book in which the theory of Bookkeeping is in harmony with actual practice. In the subsequent pages I have endeavoured to supply this want, and the result of my effort must be decided by the measure of success which the students, who study its pages, may obtain.

It only remains for me to add that the book has been written in accordance with the method I have adopted in teaching, a method which I am pleased to state has met with conspicuous success in both the Elementary and Advanced Bookkeeping Examinations of the Union of Lancashire and Cheshire Institutes.

I shall at all times be glad to consider any suggestions that may be made to me by teachers who have adopted the book for their classes.

GEO. F. CLARKE.

3 Lord Street,
    Liverpool,
        September 1898.

CONTENTS.

ERRATA.

CONTENTS.

DOUBLE ENTRY BOOKKEEPING.

CHAPTER I.

Introduction.

BOOKKEEPING has been defined by one of the most competent accountants of the present day as "the science of "correctly recording in books transactions involving the "transfer of money or money's worth." The necessity of keeping such a record of his transactions is perfectly plain to the merchant, or trader, as it enables him to ascertain :— Bookkeeping

Dicksee's Bookkeeping page 1.

1. What he owes to other people.
2. What his business consists of.
3. What profit or loss his business shows.
4. What capital he has in his business.

There are two systems of bookkeeping generally understood, although it is doubtful whether one is entitled to be described as a system at all. This latter one is called SINGLE ENTRY, so styled because every transaction is entered in the books once. In single entry only Personal Accounts are kept. By this method a merchant cannot arrive at the four objects above-named, the records of his buying and selling only being sufficient to show him :— Single entry

1. What he owes to other people.
2. What amount is owing to him.

A single entry system pure and simple would not allow a merchant to keep a Cash Book, this being a book in which the principle of DOUBLE ENTRY is adopted.

Double entry, as the name suggests, necessitates the entry of each transaction twice, in one form or another. Double entry

the top of which is written the name of the person, or other descriptive name, whose transactions will be entered in that account. The form and uses of various columns is shown by the following illustration :—

Dr. (Or debit side.) ANDREW BLACK. (Or credit side.) *Cr.*

Date	Particulars	Fo.	Amount	Date	Particulars	Fo.	Amount
1898 Jan. 1	To Goods ..	1	£ s d 10 0 0	1898 Feb. 1 June 30	By Cash on Account „ Balance ..	C. B. 3 ..	£ s d 7 10 0 2 10 0
							£10 0 0
June 30	To Balance ..	..	2 10 0				

Where one side of an account is greater than the other the difference is called the balance. If the debit side is greater then the difference is a debit balance. *Vice versa*, if the credit side is greater the difference is a credit balance.

In double entry bookkeeping the accounts may be classified under three headings, viz. :— **Three classes of accounts.**

1. Personal Accounts.
2. Real or Property Accounts.
3. Nominal or Impersonal Accounts.

Personal Accounts are those of various persons, either debtors or creditors. Andrew Black's account as above is a Personal Account. **Personal and Real Accounts.**

Real or Property Accounts include those which represent something tangible or real, something that may be converted into money or exchanged, *e.g.* :—

Goods.　　　　　　Land and buildings.
Cash.　　　　　　Fixtures and fittings.
Investments.　　　Plant and machinery.

These are a subdivision of the Profit and Loss Account (the account by which the merchant ascertains if he is making a profit or a loss), and, strictly speaking, may be said to represent the merchant himself. They include principally **Nominal or Impersonal Accounts.**

accounts which are a subdivision of his Profit and Loss
Account, so analysed that he may see how the profit or los
has been made, e.g. :—

Wages	Interest and discount
Rent, rates, and taxes	Bad debts
Depreciation	Carriage, etc., etc.

are all nominal or fictitious accounts.*

What is a Balance Sheet?

If the books of a merchant have been properly kept and
his transactions correctly entered, we shall be able to prepare
what is technically termed a Balance Sheet.   A' Balance
Sheet is a classified statement of all the balances of the
merchant's accounts, showing on the one side

(1) What property he has, including debts owing to him.
  These are called his *Assets.*

And on the other side is shown—

(2) What amount he owes to creditors.
  These are described as his *Liabilities.*

A FORM OF BALANCE SHEET.

Liabilities.	£	s	d	Assets.	£	s	d
Sundry Creditors	20	0	0	Cash in hand	5	0	0
Capital	30	0	0	Cash at bank	10	0	0
				Sundry Debtors . ..	15	0	0
				Stock on hand	20	0	0
	£50	0	0		£50	0	0

Assets and liabilities.

To decide which are assets and which are liabilities the
following simple rules are given :—

An asset is always a debit balance that will subsequently be
received by the business.

A liability is always a credit balance that the business may
subsequently have to pay.

What is capital?

A Capital Account in a merchant's books is practically the
amount his business owes to him.   This is ascertained by his

* The word fictitious is sometimes used to describe the Impersonal
Accounts connected with the Profit and Loss Account.

first finding out the total *assets* he has in his business, and by how much they exceed his *liabilities*. The excess of his assets over his liabilities is his capital. If his assets amount to £100, and his liabilities to £50, his capital would be £50, which amount would be shown in the Capital Account in the Ledger.

A Profit and Loss Account is, as the name implies, an account of the merchant's gain or loss. The form of account is the same as any other in the Ledger. The account is *debited* with all expenses incurred in the conduct of the business, and *credited* with all profit made by the business. The detailed working of a Profit and Loss Account will be more fully dealt with in a subsequent chapter. *What is a Profit and Loss Account?*

A Trial Balance (only possible in a system of double entry bookkeeping) is a detailed list of the balances of every account in the Ledger. All the debit and credit balances are placed in separate columns, and, if the work has been correctly done, the total of the debit balances, including the balance of cash in hand, will equal the total of the credit balances. This is a proof that each balance is correct as recorded in the Ledger. *What is a Trial Balance?*

Journalising is the art of recording in the Journal in chronological order all the transactions affecting the merchant's business. It also applies to the making of what are known as *opening entries, transfer entries*, and *closing entries*. For full explanation of these see Chapters II. and III. *Journalising.*

This is a phrase used to describe the operation of entering in the Ledger each transaction, previously recorded in the Journal or Cash Book. In Andrew Black's account, given on page 3, the value of goods, £10, therein debited or charged to him, is said to be posted to his account from the Journal. So with the cash paid by him, the amount of £7 10s., first entered in the Cash Book, is now posted to the credit of his account in the Ledger. *Posting into the Ledger.*

CHAPTER II

A Merchant's Books.

The books required.

THE question what books does a merchant require must always be answered according to the nature of his particular business. Experience often proves that by opening special books adapted to the character and requirements of any business much labour and time may be saved. This fact, then, prevents us giving any stereotyped list of books, but, generally, the following books would be required by a merchant whose business was of an ordinary character.

Cash Book.	Sales Day Book.
Journal.	Bought Day Book or Invoice
Ledgers (Debtors and	Book.
Creditors).	Bills Receivable Book.
Returns and Allowances	Bills Payable Book.
(Inward and Outward).	

It must be observed that in all these books the principle of double entry is adhered to, and that one or other of the four rules given on page 2 is fully complied with. Their various uses will be better understood by the student as he obtains a more complete grasp of double entry principles, but it may be pointed out that the Sales Day Book, Bought or Invoice Book, Bill Books and Returns Books are all an enlargement of the Journal, special books being required in consequence of the large number of entries that have to be made therein, and the desirability of keeping separate the different classes of transac-

tions. It also facilitates a quick analysis of a merchant's
accounts, and the totals of each book indicate, without much
labour, the extent and volume of a merchant's business, *e.g.*,
the Sales Day Book or Journal, as we may choose to call it,
containing only a record of sales, will enable him to see what
his total sales are for any given period ; and so with all the
other books, the objects for which they are used afford the
same exclusive information. As, however, this book has been
written for the purpose of assisting those who contemplate
being examined in bookkeeping by the Society of Arts, the
Union of Lancashire and Cheshire Institutes, and kindred
institutions, a detailed study of these books is not necessary,
but our consideration will be confined to three of the principal
books in every business, trading or otherwise, viz. :—

(1) The Journal.
(2) Cash Book.
(3) Ledger.

THE LEDGER AND ITS USES.

To the merchant or trader it is of the highest importance The Ledger.
that the Ledger should be well and properly kept. In it is
contained the ACCOUNTS of *all persons* with whom he has done
any business, and also others which come under the heading
of REAL Accounts and IMPERSONAL Accounts. The Ledger
may be called the keystone of the business, for into it is
posted every transaction, whether it be a sale or purchase of
goods, or the receipt or payment of cash. The form of each
Ledger Account previously given will be noted by the student,
and it is well that he should now understand how these
accounts are made up. *Nothing is entered or posted into the
Ledger that has not first been recorded in the Journal or the
Cash Book.*

(1) In a Ledger Account, the *left-hand side* is the *Debtor*
side, and here we debit the receiver by entering into his
account the amount of goods or cash *he has received from us.*

The Ledger.   (2) The *right-hand side* of a Ledger Account is the *Creditor* side, and here we credit a person's account with the amount of goods or cash we have received *from him*.

As, however, in double entry bookkeeping each amount must be entered twice, debit and credit, it follows, in connection with the two rules above, that—

(1) The *Goods Account* (which is really our Trading Account) is *debited with* all the *goods purchased*, and is *credited with* all goods sold.

(2) The Cash Account (or Cash Book, as we shall henceforth speak of it, as all cash receipts and payments are entered in a separate book) *is debited with the cash that is received*, and *is credited with the cash paid away*.

The following transactions taken from the Journal or Cash Book may be traced to their respective accounts shown below:—

1898.

Jan. 1.	Bought from A. Brown Goods value	£500 10 6
,, 2.	Sold to C. White Goods value ..	650 15 0
,, 4.	Received Cash from C. White ..	600 0 0
,. 10.	Paid Cash to A. Brown	500 10 6

Dr.   A. BROWN'S ACCOUNT.   *Cr.*

1898 Jan. 10	To Cash ..	D	£ s d 500 10 6	1898 Jan. 1	By Goods ..	A	£ s d 500 10 6

Dr.   C. WHITE'S ACCOUNT.   *Cr.*

1898 Jan. 2	To Goods ..	B	£ s d 650 15 0	1898 Jan. 4 ,, 10	By Cash .. ,, Balance ..	C ..	£ s d 600 0 0 50 15 0
							£650 15 0
,, 10	To Balance ..	..	50 15 0				

Dr.		GOODS ACCOUNT.			Cr.	The Ledger.

| 1898 Jan. 1 | To A. Brown .. | A | £ s d 500 10 6 | 1898 Jan. 2 | By C. White .. | B | £ s d 650 15 0 |

Dr.　CASH ACCOUNT.　(This account is the Cash Book.)　Cr.

1898 Jan. 4	To C. White ..	C	£ s d 600 0 0	1898 Jan. 10	By A. Brown ..	D	£ s d 500 10 6
				„ „	„ Balance ..	..	99 9 6
							£600 0 0
„ 10	To Balance ..	..	99 9 6				

The debit and credit entries of each transaction are shown by the same letter being placed in the folio column of each account.

The accounts of A. Brown and C. White and the Cash Book are now closed, and the balances are brought down, which is always done when a Profit and Loss Account and Balance Sheet are to be prepared.

It will be seen that the Goods Account has not been closed, the reason being that this account is dealt with in a different manner to the other three. Its treatment is fully explained in the chapter on Profit and Loss Accounts.

EXERCISE I.

Post into the Ledger the following transactions :—

1898.

Jan. 2.	Sold Goods to G. Carter	£110 10 0
„ 7.	Bought Goods from T. Morrison	278 14 2
„ 10.	Sold Goods to G. Carter	98 2 9
„ 31.	Bought Goods from F. Murray	50 0 0

THE JOURNAL.

In the early days of the system of double entry book-keeping, the Journal proper was a far more important book to the trader than it is at the present time. Under the old Italian method of keeping accounts, from which our present system of double entry is derived, a book was kept called the Waste Book. In this book every transaction was recorded,

The Journal. whether for the sale or purchase of goods, or the receipt or payment of cash. From this Waste Book the transactions were all passed into the Journal, and from there posted into the Ledger. In practical bookkeeping there is now no such book as a Waste Book, the various transactions being entered at once into one of the books named at the beginning of this chapter. The Journal of that day no longer occupies the position it did, and its uses to-day are limited to three :—

(1) Opening entries (journalising assets and liabilities).

(2) Transfer entries (transferring an amount from one side to the other).

(3) Closing entries (transferring all Expense Accounts and profit to Profit and Loss Account, and finally to the Capital Account).

The books used, instead of the *old Journal*, are at the same time specific Journals, whether called by the name of Sales Books, Bill Book, or Returns Book, and a student used to journalising in one book all transactions, except the receipt or payment of cash, would find no difficulty in understanding the principle of these subsidiary Journals. In this work we have only one Journal as required in Examination book-keeping, and it is used for :—

(1) Making necessary opening entries
 (*i.e.*, debiting assets and crediting liabilities and capital).

(2) Entering all purchases, sales, &c.

(3) Transferring the balances of one account to another.

(4) Making closing entries.

Note. —No cash must be entered in the Journal with the exception of opening cash and bank balances, which are posted direct to the Cash Book.

Form of Journal.

The Journal.

Date	Particulars	Folio	Dr.	Cr.
			£ s d	£ s d
Mar. 3	Goods .. .. *Dr.*	..	825 0 0	
	To W. Brown..	..	..	825 0 0
„ 7	A. Black .. .. .. *Dr.*	..	712 10 0	
	To Goods	..	..	712 10 0
„ 10	C. White .. .. .. *Dr.*	..	50 0 0	
	D. Reddy .. .. .. *Dr.*	..	100 0 0	
	To Goods	..	..	150 0 0
			£1,687 10 0	£1,687 10 0

The use of the Journal having been explained, attention is now directed to the manner in which the entries are recorded. The date of each transaction is first written at the side, and in the body of the Journal the particulars are given, showing what account must be debited, and which must be credited. The sign *Dr. follows* the account to which the debit has to be posted. The word *To precedes* the account which has to be credited. In the first money (Debtor) column are entered the amounts that follow each account that has to be debited. In the second money (Credit) column is written the amount following the account which is to be credited. The first entry in the above illustration would, before being journalised, read :—

Mar. 3. Buy Goods from W. Brown £825 0 0

As the account which is increased must be debited, and the person we buy from credited, our Journal entry must be made as given in the form of Journal above.

Mar. 7. Sell to A. Black, Goods £712 10 0

The above transaction is the reverse of the previous one. By it our goods are decreased, and we therefore *credit* the *Goods* Account and *debit* the *buyer* of the goods. This entry is also shown in the above Journal. In the column which is headed "folio," the number of the Ledger Account is entered, to which the amount has been posted. The folio (or number) of the Ledger Account, when placed in the folio column of the Journal, is a sign that the amount has been posted into the Ledger.

EXERCISE II.

Journalise and post into the Ledger :—

Jan.	3.	Bought of W. Thornton, Wine ..	..	£450 0 0
,,	7.	Sold to Jno. Cox, Wine ..	..	300 0 0
,,	10.	Sold to Thomas Boston, Wine ..	..	100 0 0
..	15.	Bought of James Bent, Wine ..	..	830 0 0
,,	20.	Sold to Samuel Walker, Wine ..	..	600 0 0
,,	,,	Sold to Frederick Briggs, Wine ..	..	250 0 0
,,	24.	Bought of Thomas Gough, Wine	..	125 0 0

EXERCISE III.

Journalise and post into the Ledger :—

Jan.	1.	Bought of J. Ling, Raisins	..	£80 0 0
,,	,,	Bought of R. Shaw, Sugar	..	216 0 0
,,	3.	Sold to F. Clarke, Raisins	..	60 0 0
,,	7.	Bought of J. Todd, Rice ..	..	75 0 0
,,	10.	Sold to J. Moses, Sugar ..	..	250 0 0
,,	31.	Sold to H. Brown, Rice ..	..	85 0 0

THE CASH BOOK.

The Cash Book.

Our next and last book of account is the Cash Book. It will be necessary for the student to give the closest attention to this book, and to follow, carefully, the entries made therein of the series of transactions in Exercise IV. The Cash Book has three money columns on each side, as will be observed from the form given on page 14. Each column is numbered 1, 2, 3 on either side, which is intended to guide the student as to the column in which the several amounts, received and paid, must be entered.

RECEIPTS SIDE OF CASH BOOK.

On this side is entered :—
Balance of cash in hand (2)
    Do.   in bank (3)
Cash received from debtors (2)
Cheques received from debtors (2)
Cash paid into bank (A) (3)
Cash received from bank (B) (2)
Discounts allowed to debtors (1)

PAYMENTS SIDE OF CASH BOOK.

On this side is entered :—
Cash paid to creditors (2)
Cheques paid to creditors (3)
Cash and cheques paid into bank (A) (2)
Discounts allowed by creditors (1)
Cash withdrawn from bank (B) (13)

EXERCISE IV.

Jan.	1.	Balance of Cash in hand	£10	0	0
,,	2.	Received Cash from C. Gould £100, and allowed him discount, £5	105	0	0
,,	3.	Paid Cash into Bank	100	0	0
,,	4.	Paid C. Brett cheque	60	0	0
,,	10.	Received cheque from T. Wilson £10 (banked same day), and allowed discount £2	42	0	0
,,	15.	Withdrew Cash from Bank	20	0	0
,,	26.	Paid T. Jones cheque £30, and was allowed discount £1 10s.	31	10	0

FORM OF CASH BOOK.

CASH (Receipts side).

		Fo.	1 Discount £ s d	2 Cash £ s d	3 Bank £ s d
Jan. 1	To Balance in hand	..	..	10 0 0	..
„ 2	„ C. Gould	..	5 0 0	100 0 0	..
„ 3	„ Cash	A.	..	..	100 0 0
„ 10	„ C. Wilson	..	2 0 0	..	40 0 0
„ 15	„ Bank	B.	..	20 0 0	..
			£7 0 0	£130 0 0	£140 0 0
„ 26	To Balance	..	..	30 0 0	30 0 0

CONTRA (Payments side).

		Fo.	1 Discount £ s d	2 Cash £ s d	3 Bank £ s d
Jan. 3	By Bank	A.	..	100 0 0	60 0 0
„ 4	„ C. Brett	B.	..	..	20 0 0
„ 15	„ Cash	..	1 10 0	..	30 0 0
„ 26	„ T. Jones	..	..	..	30 0 0
„ „	„ Balance	..	..	30 0 0	30 0 0
			£1 10 0	£130 0 0	£140 0 0

We need not explain the transactions under Exercise IV., The Cash
which are fully set forth in the form of Cash Book given above. Book.
The uses of the various columns are given at the top of each,
but the part stating what particular items should be
entered on each side should be diligently studied. It will
assist the student to understand the necessary procedure for
entering similar transactions.

The advantage of having a discount column in the Cash The discount
Book is well known to all who have to keep traders' accounts. column.
By entering the discounts in addition to the cash or cheque
received or paid the two amounts may be posted into the
Ledger to the credit or debit of the account concerned, *e.g.*, the
amount entered in above Cash Book on January 3rd from C.
Gould would be credited in the Ledger to C. Gould's Account—
By Cash, £100, Discount £5, £105. The payment to T.
Jones on January 26th would be posted to the debit of T.
Jones' Account in the Ledger—*To Cheque £30, Discount £1 10s.,
£31 10s.* The totals of the two discount columns need not be
the same, as the total on each side is posted separately. The
total on the receipts side is posted to the debit of the Discount
Account in the Ledger, and the total on the payments side to
the credit. From the discount entries in our form of Cash
Book the postings in the Ledger Account would be thus :—

Dr.		Discount Account.			*Cr.*		
	£ s d					£ s d	
To Discounts, per C.B.	7 0 0	By Discounts, per C.B.				1 10 0	

The cash columns are practically the Cash Ledger Account, Cash columns
cash being debited, and the payor credited, with what is
received, and on the payments side, cash is credited, and the
payee debited, with the amount paid to him. This principle
applies whether cash or cheques are paid, the only distinction
necessary being the columns in which the entry is made.

The totals of the cash columns must agree by the balance

being included on the payments side and brought down on the receipts side in the manner shown in our form of Cash Book.

The bank columns, the same as the cash columns, are equivalent to a Ledger Account, the column on the receipts side being the debit, and the one on the payments side the credit. The payment of a cheque, instead of cash, to a creditor presents no difficulty, the amount in either case being posted to his debit, the credit being made by the simple entry of the amount in the cash column, if cash is paid, and bank column if a cheque is given. The payments into and withdrawals from the bank are rather more confusing, and probably the student will have wondered why, in the list of entries to be made on each side of the Cash Book given on page 12, it should be stated that cash paid into the bank must be entered on the receipts as well as on the payments side. This is, however, in accordance with fact, and as the cash and bank columns represent two separate accounts, the following rules must be observed:—

1. When cash is paid into the bank.

Credit Cash and debit Bank as shown in the Cash Book entries opposite the letter *A*. This is one transaction as given in Exercise IV., on January 3.

2. When cash is withdrawn from the bank.

Credit Bank and debit Cash in the way we have dealt with the transaction in the same exercise on January 15. The letter *B* shows the debit to cash on the receipts side and the credit to bank on the payments side.

Interest allowed by the bank is entered on the receipts side in the bank column and posted to the credit of the Interest and Commission Account, the bank being debited by the amount being entered in the bank column.

Commission charged by the bank is entered on the payments side in the bank column, and posted to the debit of the Interest and Commission Account.

A separate account is opened in the Ledger for Petty Cash, Petty cash. and any payments out of this account must be first passed through the Journal, before being posted into the Ledger.

EXERCISE V.

Enter the following in the Cash Book :—

				£	s	d
Jan.	1.	Received £50 from A. Brooks and allowed				
		him discount £2 10s.		£52	10	0
,,	2.	Paid into Bank		40	0	0
,,	7.	Paid A. Robinson Cash		10	0	0
,,	10.	Withdrew from Bank		20	10	0
,,	15.	Received from Loreing & Co. cheque and				
		paid into Bank		100	0	0
,,	21.	Paid Jas. Chorlton cheque £80 and was				
		allowed discount £3		83	0	0

EXERCISE VI.

Write up and balance the Cash Book.

			£	s	d
Feb.	1.	Balance of Cash in hand	50	0	0
,,	,,	Do. at Bank	300	0	0
,,	10.	Paid A. Marshall cheque £100 and was			
		allowed discount £5	105	0	0
,,	15.	Received from Lane & Nimmo Cash £70			
		and allowed discount £3	73	0	0
,,	20.	Paid into Bank	100	0	0
,,	25.	Paid H. Fleming Cash	15	0	0
,,	28.	Withdrew from Bank	75	0	0
,,	,,	Advanced for Petty Cash	5	0	0

C

CHAPTER III.

Assets and Liabilities—Bills of Exchange—Promissory Notes and Cheques.

ASSETS AND LIABILITIES.

THE opening entries usually made in the Journal are those relating to the trader's assets and liabilities. Bearing in mind what has already been written on this head in our first chapter, we now show how these opening entries must be made. As before stated, assets are always shown in the books as debit balances and liabilities as credit balances. Whenever a list of assets are given to be journalised, and they exceed the amount of liabilities, the *difference must be credited to Capital Account.*

As—in the Journal—the accounts with debit balances are always stated first, our first entry will be

Assets *Dr.*   .To Liabilities *Cr.*,

and we then give, in their proper order, the separate balances.

EXAMPLE.

On June 30th 1882 the books of Allen & Co. were closed with the following result :—

ASSETS.			£	s	d	LIABILITIES.				£	s	d
Cash in hand	..	..	16	12	8	Bills Payable	..	..	..	329	2	9
Cash at Bank	..	..	138	12	4	Wood & Co.	..	..	..	113	13	8
Goods	..	..	1,500	0	0							
Bills Receivable	..	..	723	18	10							
Business Premises	..	..	1,200	0	0							
T. Davies	..	..	83	3	8							
Mackenzie Bros.	..	..	109	13	4							

Make the opening entries of above balances in the Journal.

JOURNAL, 30th June 1882.

							Dr. £ s d	Cr. £ s d
Sundry Assets	..	..	..	..	Dr.			
To Liabilities..	..	..	..	..	.			
Cash in hand ..	..	..	..	..	Dr.		16 12 8	
Cash at Bank ..	..	..	..	..	Dr.		138 12 4	
Goods	..	..	..	..	Dr.		1,500 0 0	
Bills Receivable	..	..	..	..	Dr.		723 18 10	
Business Premises	..	..	..	..	Dr.		1,200 0 0	
T. Davies.. ..	..	..	..	..	Dr.		83 3 8	
Mackenzie Bros. ..	..	..	..	..	Dr.		109 13 4	
To Bills Payable	..	..	..	..	Cr.		..	329 2 9
„ Wood & Co.	..	..	..	..	Cr.		..	113 13 8
„ Capital Account	..	..	..	..	Cr.		..	3,329 4 5

These Journal entries will now be posted into their respective accounts :—

The cash in hand
and
The cash at bank } each into their respective columns in the Cash Book,

The remaining balances into their separate Ledger Accounts.

Debit and credit amounts in the Journal appear as debits and credits in the Cash Book and Ledger Accounts.

EXERCISE VII.

Assets and liabilities of Richard Bright on 31st December 1887 :—

He owed

P. Wilkins	..	..	..	..	..	..	£240 10 0
F. Davis	..	..	..	..	..	..	150 7 9
Wright & Co. ..	..	..	..	..	..		78 15 3
C. Dickins	..	..	..	..	..	..	305 0 0
On Bills payable	..	..	..	..	..		689 3 2

He had

Cash at Office ..	..	..	..	..	..		£342 10 0
Cash at Bank ..	..	..	..	..	..		1,600 0 0
Petty Cash	..	..	..	..	..	..	2 3 6
Bills Receivable	..	..	..	..	..		549 18 5
Wine	..	..	..	..	..		6,859 0 0
Spirits	..	..	..	..	..		1,215 10 0
Business Premises	..	..	..	..	..		600 0 0
T. King owed him	..	..	..	..	..		265 10 0
J. Jackson owed him ..	..	..	..	..			75 9 6
S. Johnstone owed him	..	..	..	..			183 12 10
B. Hare owed him	..	..	..	..	..		315 14 11

Make the necessary opening entries in the Journal.

BILLS OF EXCHANGE.

The definition of a bill of exchange in the Bills of Exchange Act 1882 is as follows :—

" A bill of exchange is an unconditional order in writing " addressed by one person to another, signed by the person " giving it, requiring the person to whom it is addressed to " pay on demand, or at a fixed or determinable future time, a " sum certain in money to, or to the order of, a specified " person or to bearer" (section 1). Bills of exchange are drawn in various forms, the one mostly used being as under :—

FORM OF BILL.

£100   *Liverpool, 1st January 1898.*
(Stamp 1s.)

Accepted, payable at Lloyd's Bank. **BLACK & WHITE.** *1 Jan. 1898.*

Three months after date pay A. B., or order, the sum of One hundred pounds sterling for value received.

                                 C. D.

To Messrs. Black & White,
          Manchester.

The parties to this bill are three :—The drawer, *C. D.*, the payee, *A. B.*, the drawees, *Messrs. Black & White.* When the bill is accepted by Messrs. Black & White they become acceptors, *i.e.,* they agree to do what the drawer C. D. requires. Thenceforward the bill is styled Messrs. Black & White's acceptance. Before being accepted by them it is called C. D.'s draft. A bill is accepted by the drawee writing across the face of the bill in the manner shown on the above form. When these formalities are completed the bill becomes, to the drawer C. D., a bill receivable ; to the acceptors, Messrs. Black & White, a bill payable. After acceptance C. D. would enter the bill in his Bills Receivable Book, and in his Journal would credit Messrs. Black & White by making the following entry :—

Jan. 1.   Bill Receivable, *Dr.*   ..   £100   0   0
       To Black & White   ..   £100   0   0

In the case of C. D. accepting a draft from Messrs. Black & White, that becomes a bill *payable* by him, and after entering particulars of the bill in his Bills Payable Book would make the following Journal entry:—

Jan. 1. Black & White, *Dr.* .. £100 0 0
   To Bill Payable .. £100 0 0

When the time named in a bill has expired, and three extra days, called days of grace, have elapsed, the bill is presented for payment at the place named on the bill. In the form above the bill is payable at Lloyds' Bank, and on the 4th April 1898 we call there with the bill, or, it may be presented by our bankers, and if the acceptor has sufficient money in the bank we obtain cash for it. This is called honouring the bill. C. D. would then enter the amount in his Cash Book on the receipts side to the credit of Bills Receivable Account in the Ledger (not Black & White's account, as they were credited when they gave the bill), as under:—

CASH.   CONTRA.
1898
April 4. To Bill Receivable—
   Black & White's
      acceptance £100 0 0

Should C. D. have to meet a bill, *i.e.*, pay it when it becomes due, his Cash Book entry would be on the payments side, when the amount would be entered to the debit of Bills Payable Account, as follows:—

CASH.   CONTRA.
   April 4. By Bills Pay-
      able .. £100 0 0

A bill of exchange when presented for payment may be what is technically termed dishonoured, *i.e.*, payment of it is refused. The acceptor may not have sufficient money in the bank to cover the amount of the bill, in which event certain formalities have to be gone through. The person who has presented the bill for payment must have the bill noted, or

protested for non-payment before a notary. Notice of the
bill being dishonoured must be given to the parties concerned,
and the following entry made in the Journal :—

> April 4. Black & White, *Dr.*   ..   £100 0 0
>   To Bill Receivable   .. ·   £100 0 0
>   For their acceptance returned dishonoured.

Messrs. Black & White would also have to pay any expenses
that had been incurred by the dishonouring of the bill, which
would be debited to their account through the Cash Book.

Discounting
bills.

A bill is discounted by payment being obtained before it is
due. The discount is the charge made by the bank for giving
the holder of the bill the necessary accommodation. When a
bill is discounted it is entered in the Cash Book in the same
way as if payment had been made by the drawer, the discount being entered in the discount column, and the net cash
received in the cash column, the total being posted to the
credit of Bills Receivable Account. To take up, or to retire a
bill, is to pay cash when the bill is presented for payment.

Promissory Notes and Cheques.

Promissory
notes.

A promissory note is treated in our Journal as a bill
receivable or payable, according to whether we are to
receive or to pay the amount named in the note. In form,
however, it is different to a bill of exchange, being defined in
the Act of 1882 (Bills of Exchange) as " An unconditional
" promise in writing made by one person to another, signed by
" the maker, engaging to pay on demand or at a fixed or
" determinable future time a sum certain in money to or to
" the order of a specified person or to bearer." In this
case there is no need for the note to be accepted by the
person who will ultimately have to pay the money, the mere
fact of his signing the note making him liable for the sum
stated therein. The only person named in the note beside the
payor is the payee, *i.e.*, the person to whom the note is

addressed, or named in the body of it, while the parties to a bill are generally three, viz., drawer, acceptor, and payee.

FORM OF PROMISSORY NOTE.

£100. *Liverpool, 1 January 1898.*

On demand (or three months after date) I promise to pay C. F. or order (or bearer) one hundred pounds.

A. E.

A cheque, although only an order on a bank to pay a stated Cheques. amount to a person named in the cheque, is dealt with in the books of account as if it were cash. Cheques are made payable either to bearer or order. A bearer cheque entitles *the holder* to receive the cash, while an order cheque must be *endorsed* by the person, to whom it is payable, writing his name on the back before the bank will pay the money.

A cheque is crossed *generally* by drawing two parallel lines Crossed across the face of it, and writing " & Co." between them. The cheques. effect of crossing a cheque in this way is to allow payment of the cheque only through the medium of a banker. The words " Not negotiable " are also sometimes written across, which gives additional safety to a cheque, as any person receiving such a cheque can only take it with the same title as the transferor possessed. Cheques are *specially* crossed when a banker's name is written between the parallel lines, and when this is done payment will only be made through that banker.

EXERCISE VIII.

Enter the following transactions in their proper books of account :—

April	5.	Received from J. Hill, his acceptance ..	£150	0	0
,,	7.	Accepted T. Jones' draft at 3 months ..	200	0	0
,,	10.	Received from H. Clarke, his draft on S. Howarth	300	0	0
,,	15.	Gave A. White Promissory Note.. ..	250	0	0
July	8.	Received Cash for J. Hills' acceptance ..	150	0	0
,,	10.	Met T. Jones' draft due this day	200	0	0
,,	13.	Received Cash for S. Howarth's acceptance	300	0	0
,,	31.	Paid amount of Promissory Note given to A. White	250	0	0

CHAPTER IV.

Trading Account—Goods Account—Profit and Loss Account—Trial Balance—Balance Sheet.

IN practical bookkeeping the account by which a merchant ascertains his gross profit is called a Trading Account, *i.e.*, a record of his business transactions, leaving out the expenses that have been incurred in the conduct of such trade. The profit shown by this account can then only be the gross profit, and the balance is transferred, through the medium of the Journal, to the credit of the Profit and Loss Account. There is some difference of opinion as to how a Trading Account should be prepared in its strictest sense, but the one most generally adopted includes the following particulars :—

TRADING ACCOUNT.

Debit.	£	s	d	*Credit.*	£	s	d
Stock on hand at commencement of Trading Period				Total Sales during Period of Trading			
Total Purchases of Stock since do.				Stock on hand at the end of			
Balance—Gross Profit				Trading Period			

It is not, however, our intention to discuss in detail the method of working such an account as this, seeing that in our *Goods Account* we are able to obtain exactly the same result as can be shown by a Trading Account. Reference to it is only made for the information of the student in order that he might understand that in practical bookkeeping a distinction is drawn between a Trading Account and a Profit and Loss Account. The difference is really only in name, as the final balance of each of these accounts shows either a profit or loss. To the merchant the value of a Trading Account lies in the fact that he can see the result of his business on his buying and selling alone.

This information our Goods Account will give us, and it is Goods Account. to this account that we must turn for a record of all our purchases and sales. There are also other small items entered in our Goods Account that a merchant would not put into his Trading Account, such as carriage on goods bought. This is done because a Goods Account must be debited with the total cost of the goods, and where carriage has to be paid, in addition to the purchase price, it is evident that the amount so paid must be added before we can get at our total cost. In like manner, all freight paid, a term used to imply the cost of conveying goods by ship from one port to another, is added to the purchase price of the goods in respect of which the freight is charged, by being debited to the Goods Account.

From the particulars given above as to how a Trading Account is generally made up, we have an insight into the composition of our Goods Account, which will be more fully explained by the Goods Account that is shown below, prepared from the following transactions:—

1898.					
Jan. 1.	Stock on hand at commencement	..	£550	0	0
,, ,,	Purchased Goods for cash	..	500	0	0
,, ,,	Paid Freight on above purchase..	..	12	0	0
,, 5.	Sold C. Donem Goods value	..	350	0	0
,, 10.	Sold D. Simple Goods	..	500	0	0
,, 15.	Bought Goods from A. Piper	..	600	0	0
,, ,,	Paid Carriage on same	..	17	10	0
,, 20.	Sold Goods for cash	..	750	10	0
,, 25.	Bought Goods from B. Long	..	200	0	0
,, 31.	Stock on hand at this date	..	650	0	0

Note.—It must be borne in mind that although a Goods Account only is given here, the above transactions are supposed to have first been passed through either the Cash Book or Journal.

Dr.					GOODS ACCOUNT.					Cr.

1898				£	s	d	1898			£	s	d
Jan. 1	To Stock on hand	..		550	0	0	Jan. 5	By C. Donem, Goods J	350	0	0
„ „	„ Cash for Goods	C		500	0	0	„ 10	„ D. Simple, „ J	500	0	0
„ „	„ Freight	C		12	0	0	„ 20	„ Cash for Goods C	750	10	0
„ 15	„ A. Piper, Goods	J		600	0	0			£1,600	10	0
„ „	„ Cash, Carriage	C		17	10	0					
„ 25	„ B. Long, Goods	J		200	0	0					
				£1,879	10	0	„ 31	„ Stock on hand ..	650	0	0
„ 31	„ Gross Profit, transferred to Profit and Loss Account			371	0	0					
				£2,250	10	0			£2,250	10	0
„ 31	To Stock on hand brought down	..		650	0	0					

Dr. entries. To take the above series of entries separately, we have first in order the stock on hand at the commencement of our trading period. This is always the first debit to the Goods Account, except in a new business. The remaining debit entries included in the total of £1,879 10s. represent purchases and carriage on same, which, again, are always debited to the Goods Account.

Credit entries. On the credit side we have a total of £1,600 10s., which represents sales during the month, SALES being always credited to the Goods Account.

Stock on hand. Before the gross profit can be known the stock on hand must first be credited in the Goods Account. No Journal entry is necessary in this case, the amount being recorded straightway in the account as shown above. After the stock on hand has been credited, if the credit side is still the greater, the balance is gross profit ; if the debit side predominates the result is a loss.

Gross Profit. The above account shows that a gross profit of £371 has been made, and as in making out a Profit and Loss Account the Goods Account must be closed, *i.e.*, the totals of both sides agreed, and the account ruled off, a Journal entry will be necessary, which we make as under :—

Jan. 31. Goods Account, *Dr.* .. £371 0 0
     To Profit & Loss Account, *Cr.*| £371 0 0
   For gross profit transferred to latter account.

The Goods Account is thereby closed, and we have only to take it into further consideration so far as regards the stock on hand. After the stock on hand has been credited, and the Goods Account closed, the stock is carried down to the *debit* side, and, as representing an asset (a balance which will subsequently be received by the business), it will be brought into our Balance Sheet. *(margin: Bringing down stock on hand.)*

A Profit and Loss Account when finally completed shows the ultimate profit or loss which the business has made. To this account all *loss is debited*, and *gain credited*. The profit made, as per our Goods Account shown above, will be *credited*, from the Journal where the transfer entry has been made, to Profit and Loss Account. We have explained that in the course of a merchant's business he opens various Nominal Accounts in his Ledger, to which he posts the different items of expense, including salaries, rent, interest, bad debts, insurance, and depreciation, which have to be deducted from whatever profit has been made. Separate accounts are first opened for each class of expenses, and when the books are being closed, the totals of these Nominal or Expense Accounts are transferred to the debit of Profit and Loss Account, in the same way as the balance of Goods Account is transferred to the credit. *(margin: Profit and Loss Account.)*

Assuming the following to be balances of their respective Ledger Accounts at the end of a given period :—

Rent, Rates and Taxes, debit	..	..	..	..	£10 0 0
Salaries and Wages, debit	..	..	..	..	35 0 0
Interest and Discount, debit	..	..	..	..	17 10 0
Bad Debts, debit ..	..	..	..	..	20 0 0
Commission, credit..	..	..	..	..	35 0 0
Trade Charges, debit	..	..	..	..	7 10 0

they will be transferred by making entries in the Journal, usually termed the closing entries, as follows :—

CLOSING JOURNAL ENTRIES.

Transfer of
Nominal
Accounts,

		Folio	Dr.	Cr.
			£ s d	£ s d
Jan. 31	Profit and Loss .. .. *Dr.*	..	90 0 0	
	To Sundries			
	To Rent, Rates and Taxes..	..	..	10 0 0
	„ Salaries and Wages	..	..	35 0 0
	„ Interest and Discount	..	..	17 10 0
	„ Bad Debts	..	..	20 0 0
	„ Trade Charges	..	..	7 10 0
Jan. 31	Commission .. .. *Dr.*	..	35 0 0	
	To Profit and Loss	..	..	35 0 0
			£125 0 0	£125 0 0

Dr.   PROFIT AND LOSS ACCOUNT.   *Cr.*

Compiled from balances of Accounts as above, and Goods Account.

		£ s d			£ s d
Jan. 31	To Rent, Rates and Taxes	10 0 0	Jan. 31	By Goods A/c ..	371 0 0
„ „	„ Salaries and Wages	35 0 0	„ „	„ Commission ..	35 0 0
„ „	„ Interest, &c. ..	17 10 0			
„ „	„ Bad Debts ..	20 0 0			
„ „	„ Trade Charges	7 10 0			
„ „	„ Capital A/c ..	316 0 0			
		£ 406 0 0			£ 406 0 0

Closing Profit
and Loss
Account.

One further entry is now required to close the Profit and Loss Account, which is done by transferring the net profit of £316, this being the excess of credits over the debits, to the credit of the merchant's Capital Account.

JOURNAL ENTRY.

Profit and Loss Account, *Dr*...   ..   £316   0   0

     To Capital Account £316   0   0

Net profit as per Profit and Loss Account transferred to credit of Capital.

TRIAL BALANCE.

Trial
Balance.

The note in the opening chapter, defining a Trial Balance, will not be sufficient to give the student a fair idea of how the Trial Balance must be made. This is usually done after the Journal and Cash Book have been posted, and before the

Ledger Accounts are closed. It is only safe to close the accounts after the Trial Balance has been got out, as, if any amounts have been posted wrongly, and the balances of the accounts entered and ruled off, the errors will have to be rectified, thereby giving more trouble than if the balances had been first tested. The balances will be entered in the debit or credit column of the Trial Balance, and if they are correct the two columns will total to the same amount. After the Trial Balance has been prepared the Goods Account will be closed by crediting the stock on hand to find out the gross profit. This will be transferred to the Profit and Loss Account, as shown on page 27. The balances of the Nominal Accounts appearing in the Trial Balance are then transferred through the Journal, in the same way, to the Profit and Loss Account, which is explained at length in this chapter.

Trial Balance.

FORM OF TRIAL BALANCE FROM PAPER SET BY LONDON CHAMBER OF COMMERCE.

	Debit Balances	Credit Balances
	£ s d	£ s d
Sales	..	98,599 17 7
A. Jones—Capital	..	14,000 0 0
Stationery and Printing	189 19 7	
Travelling Expenses	18 0 0	
Sundry Debtors	8,216 1 1	
Trade Expenses	359 10 5	
Stock on hand, *1st January 1893*	2,226 4 6	
Cash in hand	19 1 1	
Cash at Bank	3,621 11 2	
Law Expenses..	14 3 9	
Wages	4,670 4 7	
Purchases	85,786 1 0	
Salaries	1,936 13 10	
Plant, Furniture, &c.	4,209 10 5	
A. Jones—Current Account	3,200 0 0	
Discounts	1,259 13 10	
Rent, Rates, and Taxes	994 4 10	
Sundry Creditors	..	4,121 2 6
	£116,721 0 1	£116,721 0 1

Stock on hand, 31st December 1893, £1,931 10s. 3d.

Make closing Journal entries from above Trial Balance.

BALANCE SHEET.

After the Nominal Accounts have been transferred to the Profit and Loss Account, and the balance of net profit trans-

Balance Sheet.

Balance
Sheet.

ferred to Capital Account, the balances remaining in their respective Ledger Accounts will represent either assets or liabilities. From these we prepare our Balance Sheet in the manner shown in our opening chapter. It may cause the student some surprise to find that a debit balance in a Ledger Account, *i.e.*, an asset, is placed on the credit side in the Balance Sheet. This need not cause any alarm, as it is a form of account to which he will quickly adapt himself. A full and explanatory Balance Sheet is given on page 67. In preparing a Balance Sheet the assets and liabilities should be arranged in the following order :—

Order of
liabilities and
assets.

Liabilities.	*Assets.*
Sundry Creditors.	Cash in hand.
Bills Payable.	Cash at Bank.
Capital Account.	Petty Cash.
	Sundry Debtors.
	Bills Receivable.
	Fixtures and Fittings.
	Plant, &c.
	Stock on hand.

EXERCISE IX.

London Chamber of Commerce.

1895.

			£	s.	d.
Jan.	1.	B. Jones commences business with £300, which he pays into a Bank	£300	0	0
,,	,,	Buys Goods of H. Brown	80	0	0
,,	2.	Pays H. Brown cheque for £76 6s. 8d. and was allowed discount of £3 13s. 4d.	80	0	0
,,	5.	Buys Goods of J. Rook	110	8	6
,,	6.	Sells Goods to O. Smith	106	10	8
,,	7.	Buys Goods of H. Brown	230	8	10
,,	9.	Draws cheque in favour of J. Rook ..	50	0	0
,,	10.	Sells Goods to M. Jenks	100	0	0
,,	11.	Receives cheque from O. Smith for ..	106	10	8
,,	14.	Draws cheque for Wages	32	15	0
,,	19.	Receives cheque from M. Jenks £97 8s. 6d. and allowed him discount £2 11s. 6d.	100	0	0

EXERCISE IX.—*continued.*

1895.

Jan,	24.	Sells Goods to O. Smith ..	..	..	109	11	10
„	29.	Draws Cash from Bank ..	..	..	60	0	0
„	„	Pays Wages	..	..	32	0	0
„	„	Pays Rent	..	..	20	0	0
„	31.	Receives Cash from O. Smith ..	..		75	0	0
„	„	Draws Cash on Private Account ..	..		30	0	0
„	„	Pays Cash into Bank ..	..	..	30	0	0
„	„	Stock on hand at this date	..	..	275	0	0

Write up the Journal and Cash Book from above Exercise. Post into Ledger, prepare Trial Balance, Profit and Loss Account, and Balance Sheet.

CHAPTER V.

Partnership Accounts—Current Accounts—Joint Ventures—Consignments.

Partnership Accounts.
WHERE two or more persons (but not exceeding 20, the maximum number allowed by the Partnership Act 1890 for trading concerns) are engaged in the same business, and sharing its profits in accordance with a written or verbal agreement, the business is a partnership one, in which various matters have to be taken into consideration that do not enter into a business worked by one individual. In one respect private and partnership businesses are the same, *i.e.*, trade is done and business carried on in the same way. One set of accounts is kept of the trading, and it is only when the books are about to be closed that the matters referred to above receive prominent attention.

Partnership Agreement.
When two or more persons contemplate commencing business together they agree upon certain conditions that are to guide them in the conduct of the business. These are usually written out at length and signed by each partner. This document is called the partnership agreement or articles of partnership ; they are thenceforth bound by it until the partnership ceases to exist, either by mutual arrangement or by the expiration of the time the partnership was to be continued.

Separate Capital Accounts.
It will be found necessary, in order to show the amount each partner has in the business, to keep a separate Capital Account for each of them. This account is not disturbed in any way until the year of business is ended, no payments made to any partner being posted to his Capital Account.

Partners usually withdraw a certain sum from the business at stated periods on account of their private expenses. The amount paid is posted from the Cash Book to the debit of the partner's Drawing, or Current, Account, which is opened in the Ledger, in addition to a Capital Account. A sum withdrawn on account of profits is also entered to the partner's Current Account, and remains debited there until the profit or loss has been ascertained. The share of profit each partner is to receive is transferred, through the Journal, to the credit of his Current Account. So, too, any interest which he receives on his capital in the business is credited to his Current Account, and where he is charged interest on his drawings, this is debited to his Current Account; the balance of the Current Account is then transferred to the Capital Account, which shows the net capital each partner has in the business. *Drawing or Current Accounts.*

JOURNAL ENTRY TRANSFERRING BALANCE OF CURRENT ACCOUNT TO CAPITAL ACCOUNT.

A. Jones, Current Account .. *Dr.* £250 0 0
    To A. Jones, Capital Account .. £250 0 0
For balance transferred to credit
  of Capital Account.

JOINT VENTURES.

A joint venture is an agreement by two or more persons to participate in a transaction in which certain risks are undertaken. The profit or loss arising out of the venture will be divided. It is necessary to keep a separate account of joint ventures, or speculations, as they have been termed, and to debit them with— *Joint ventures.*

    The cost of the goods,
    All expenses, carriage, etc.,

and credit Joint Account with

    The amount realised by the sale of the goods.

The profit or loss is then transferred to the credit or debit of the account of each adventurer by the following Journal entry, supposing a profit to have been realised :—

Jan. 31. Joint Account .. *Dr.* £250 0 0			
To D. Brown, one-half share of net profit ..		£125 0 0	
To B. White, the like ..		125 0 0	

Where an outside person participates in a joint transaction, he usually pays to the firm managing the business one-half of the cost of the goods bought on the Joint Account. This sum is entered in the Cash Book and posted to the credit of his Private Account in the Ledger, pending the result of the venture being ascertained. When this is done the amount is repaid to him, together with his share of the profit.

CONSIGNMENTS.

Consignments of two kinds.   These are of two kinds, viz., outward consignments and inward consignments. Their treatment in books of account is essentially different, the first being practically a private venture, the second representing only goods received, as consignee, to be sold on commission for the consignor, at his risk.

Outwards.   Where a trader sends goods to be sold on his behalf he is called the consignor; the person to whom he sends them is the consignee. A Consignment Account is opened, which is debited with the value of the goods, and Goods Account is credited. The Consignment Account is also debited with the carriage or freight paid, and with any charges that are incurred in connection therewith.

When the goods consigned have been realised by the consignee he is debited personally with the sum for which they have been sold, and the Consignment Account is credited. The commission, or brokerage, to be paid to the consignee is credited to his Private Account, and the Consignment Account is debited. If, after these entries have been made, the credit side of the Consignment Account is the greater, the result is a profit, while, if the debits exceed the credits, the difference is a loss, the balance in either case then being transferred to the Profit and Loss Account.

EXAMPLE.

Jan. 1. Send Goods to G. Dun to be sold on my
account and risk £300 0 0
" " Pay Carriage thereon 3 10 0

Journal Entry.

Consignment to G. Dun..*Dr.* £300 0 0
    To Goods Account .. £300 0 0

Cash Entry.

CASH. CONTRA.

    By Consignment to
    G. Dun, Carriage. £3 10 0

Jan. 10. Receive Account Sales from G. Dun—
    Goods realised £370 0 0
    His Charges and Commission .. 18 10 0

Journal Entries.

Consignment to G. Dun..*Dr.* £18 10 0
    To G. Dun £18 10 0
Commission on Sale of Goods.

G. Dun .. .. .. *Dr.* £370 0 0
    To Consignment to G. Dun £370 0 0

Consignment to G. Dun *Dr.* £48 0 0
    To Profit and Loss Account £48 0 0
Profit on Consignment transferred.

Inward consignments are goods received by a trader to be **Inwards.** sold for the consignor. When received no entry is made in the books, as the consignee does not become debtor to the consignor until he has sold the goods. When the goods are sold he debits the buyer and credits the consignor. The commission and charges are then entered to the debit of the consignor, and credited to the consignee's Commission Account, the balance then remaining due to the consignor

D

being remitted to him.   His account would thus be closed,
the transaction being duly completed.   Expenses paid on
goods before realisation are debited to the consignor.

EXERCISE X.

1898.

June	1.	T. Brick and A. Stone commence business with a capital of £1,000 in equal shares	£1,000	0	0
,,	,,	Pay into Union Bank	900	0	0
,,	2.	Bought Office Furniture for cheque	50	0	0
,,	3.	Buy Goods for cheque	800	0	0
,,	6.	Sell Goods to B. Wood	300	0	0
,,	,,	Buy Goods from T. Slater on joint account with S. Chimp	500	0	0
,,	7.	Pay Carriage on same	10	0	0
,,	,,	Receive from S. Chimp his share of joint account	250	0	0
,,	8.	Consign Goods to P. Dorner to be sold on our account	400	0	0
,,	,,	Pay Charges on same	7	10	0
,,	10.	Sold Goods bought on joint account for cash	600	0	0
,,	12.	Pay T. Slater	500	0	0
,,	18.	Receive Account Sales of Consignment to P. Dorner	500	0	0
,,	20.	Receive Cheque from P. Dorner on account (banked same day)	400	0	0
,,	,,	P. Dorner's Commission	25	0	0
,,	22.	T. Brick withdrew from bank	20	0	0
,,	,,	A. Stone do.	20	0	0
,,	25.	Buy Goods from A. Winder	250	0	0
,,	30.	Pay Clerks' Salaries	15	0	0
,,	,,	Stock on hand	500	0	0

Write up the above transactions in the Journal and Cash
Book. Post into Ledger to proper accounts, prepare Trial
Balance, Profit and Loss Account, and Balance Sheet.

CHAPTER VI.

Insolvent Debtors—Composition—Depreciation— Reserve Account—Sinking Fund.

WHERE a debtor finds that his liabilities exceed his assets, Insolvent he is insolvent, *i.e.*, he is unable to pay his creditors, and he debtors. probably becomes a bankrupt. If on the realisation of a bankrupt's estate a dividend, or payment on account of the debt, is received, that will be passed to his credit, while the balance owing, which will not be received in the future, will be written off, *i.e.*, transferred to Bad Debts Account. Where no dividend is received from a bankrupt's estate the whole debt is written off as bad.

In many cases, where a trader finds that he is insolvent, Composition. instead of filing his petition in bankruptcy, he calls a meeting of his creditors. He lays before them a statement of his affairs which shows what property he is possessed of, and what he owes to creditors. He makes a formal offer of —— shillings in the £, which, if accepted, discharges the whole of his debt. The result to the creditor is the same as if the debtor had become a bankrupt, and the balance of the debt is treated in the same way as described in the paragraph on insolvent debtors.

Where a debtor transfers his property, by deed, to a trustee Deed of to be sold by him for the benefit of his creditors, the deed is assignment. called a deed of assignment. The amount realised, less expenses, is divided amongst the creditors, a dividend being paid in the same manner as if the debtor had become bankrupt or paid a composition.

Depreciation. This term, sometimes called "wear and tear," is used to describe a decrease in the value of assets, due to their continual use or decay. In a manufacturing business, depreciation, of assets used in the process of manufacture, should be charged against the goods made—as an item in the cost of production. Where the business is not a manufacturing or productive one, depreciation of any assets may be charged against profit and loss. The Journal entry required to write off depreciation is as follows :—

Depreciation	Dr. £50 0 0			
To Leasehold Premises ..	..	£25	0	0
„ Plant and Fittings ..	..	20	0	0
„ Office Furniture ..	..	5	0	0
For depreciation of above assets.				

The total of Depreciation Account is afterwards transferred to debit of Profit and Loss Account.

It is important, in preparing Profit and Loss Accounts, that depreciation should always be charged, as otherwise, in dividing the profit, the capital may be unknowingly distributed· To avoid the question of wear and tear continually may eventually lead to bankruptcy.

Reserve Account. A Reserve Account is created by setting aside a proportion of profits for a general or specific purpose. A general reserve is one which provides for every kind of contingency; a specific reserve is one created for a special purpose, such as Reserve for Bad and Doubtful Debts. Specific Reserve Accounts should only be utilised for the purpose for which they were created. A Reserve Account appears as a liability in the Balance Sheet.

Sinking fund. A Sinking Fund is formed out of profits to provide against the loss of some particular asset, or to prepare for a liability that will ultimately have to be discharged. In the former case, where leasehold property has been purchased, and which will in due course fall into the possession of other persons by the lease expiring, the amount paid for the premises will be written over the period which the lease has still to run. The fund thus provided can be used either to purchase fresh premises, or to renew the lease of the old buildings. In the latter case, where a liability will, at an agreed date, have to be met, a sinking fund is formed to provide the amount so payable out of profits. This is usually done where debentures have been issued, which are secured on assets of a wasting nature.

Exercise XI.

Write up Cash Book and Journal. Post into Ledger. Prepare Trial Balance, Profit and Loss Account, and Balance Sheet.

On 1st January 1898 the Assets and Liabilities of A. Ward and D. Bard were as follows :—

	£	s	d		£	s	d
Cash at Bank	946	0	0	Bills Payable	1,826	15	9
Cash in hand	41	3	8	Cook & Co. ..	304	7	6
Stock-in-Trade	2,847	10	6	G. Burford ..	482	9	7
Bills Receivable	345	9	6	A. Ward, Capital	1,175	2	5
Horses and Carts	187	4	0	D. Bard, "	1,175	2	5
B. Beauchamp	36	0	0				
D. Drummond	560	10	0				
	£4,963	17	8		£4,963	17	8

Profits divided equally between partners.

			£	s	d
Jan.	1.	Received of D. Drummond, on account ..	£410	0	0
„	2.	Paid Cash into bank	400	0	0
„	3.	Paid Acceptance by cheque	630	0	0
„	4.	Received of D. Drummond and paid into bank	145	0	0
		Allowed him discount	5	10	0
„	„	Bought Goods of S. Smeaton	500	0	0
„	7.	Shipped to T. Wren, Rouen, Consignment of Goods	96	5	0
		Paid freight and insurance thereon ..	4	17	6
„	8.	Paid Rent, Rates and Taxes, cheque ..	25	10	0
„	10.	Received payment of bill per bank ..	201	9	6
„	11.	Paid Cook & Co. cheque, £288; allowed discount, £16 7s. 6d.	304	7	6
„	12.	Sold C. Caustic, Goods	600	0	0

Jan.	14.	Received from T. Wren, Rouen, Account			
		Sales £54 1 0			
		Less Commission and			
		Charges 8 2 6			
		and draft at 7 days' sight	45	18	4
,,	,,	Sold D. Drummond, Goods	700	0	0
,,	15.	Accepted S. Smeaton's draft at 3 months	500	0	0
,,	17.	Accepted composition of 15s. in £ on debt			
		due from B. Beauchamp	27	0	0
,,	24.	Wrote off value of Horse killed	37	10	0
,,	,,	Bought Goods of Cook & Co.	500	0	0
,,	,,	Drew for private use, by			
		cheque, A. Ward .. £50 0 0			
,,	,,	Drew for private use, by			
		cheque, D. Bard .. £50 0 0			
			100	0	0
,,	30.	Salaries paid by cash	20	0	0
,,	31.	Depreciation of Horses and Carts	15	0	0
,,	,,	Wrote off for future Bad Debts	50	0	0
,,	,,	Stock on hand at this date..	2,750	10	0

CHAPTER VII.

Manufacturers' Accounts—Contracts—Balancing the Accounts.

THE accounts of a manufacturer differ in detail from the accounts of an ordinary trader. The difference is not far to seek, for whereas an ordinary trader confines his business to buying and selling goods, a manufacturer makes the goods he sells, buying only the material which he subsequently converts into saleable articles. In accounts of this class there are items that do not appear in a trader's accounts. If the manufacturer only buys materials to be made into goods, it is clear that wages will have to be paid to the workmen he engages to make them. He further requires the aid of machinery and plant to assist him in the manufacture of goods. It is, therefore, necessary for the manufacturer to keep what are termed

COST ACCOUNTS.

The record of these accounts enables the manufacturer to fix the selling price of the goods, as from his books he can readily see what it has cost to make them. We cannot be expected to go into the question of Cost Accounts in an elementary treatise on bookkeeping, especially as there are matters connected therewith about which some difference of opinion exists. It will, we think, be sufficient to point out to the student that in Cost Accounts care should be taken to correctly ascertain

1. The value of the raw material used.
2. The wages paid to workmen.
3. The depreciation of machinery and plant used in the manufacture of the goods.

A mistake on the wrong side in the first two items may result in a considerable loss to the manufacturer, due to the fixing of a selling price lower than would have been fixed if the precise cost of manufacture had been correctly known at the outset.

Manu-facturing Accounts. As, however, in various examination papers questions are set which require a knowledge of Manufacturing Accounts, a simple form of setting these out is given in this chapter. It is advisable to keep the various subsidiary accounts, such as Productive Wages, Material, &c., separate, and instead of opening a separate Manufacturing Account, to open a Manu-facturing and Trading Account, to which the balances of the subsidiary accounts will be transferred. As an example, let us take a series of transactions arising out of a miller's corn and flour business :—

March 1.	He has Wheat on hand	..	..	£1,500 0 0
„ 31.	During the month he purchases Wheat value..	..	..	2,500 0 0
„ „	Wages of persons employed at Mill			70 0 0
„ „	Freight and Wharf Charges on Wheat			55 0 0
„ „	Depreciation of Mill Machinery	..		25 0 0
„ „	Total Sales of Flour to Customers	..		3,500 0 0
„ „	Stock of Wheat on hand	..	..	1,200 0 0

Instead of preparing our Trading Account of above trans-actions, as suggested in the chapter on this subject, we include the different amounts for wages, freight, &c., the complete account being as follows :—

Dr.   MANUFACTURING AND TRADING ACCOUNT.   Cr.

		£ s d			£ s d
Mar. 1	To Stock on hand ..	1,500 0 0	Mar. 31	By Sales of Flour ..	3,500 0 0
„ 31	„ Purchases of Wheat	2,500 0 0	„ „	„ Stock of Wheat on hand at cost ..	1,200 0 0
„ „	„ Wages	70 0 0			
„ „	„ Freight, &c. ..	55 0 0			
„ „	„ Depreciation of Machinery	25 0 0			
„ „	„ Gross Profit trans-ferred to Profit and Loss Account	550 0 0			
	£	4,700 0 0		£	4,700 0 0
Mar. 31	To Stock on hand, brought down	1,200 0 0			

Wherever expenditure or loss is incurred in a process of manufacture the amount must be charged to the debit of *that account*, which is credited with the sale of the goods manufactured.

Where the value of stock on hand at the *date of valuation* is lower than actual cost, the market price should be taken as the value of the stock unsold.

CONTRACTS.

A similar class of accounts to the one we have just considered is that of contracts. A contract is an agreement made between two or more persons (to carry out the provisions contained in the agreement), enforceable at law. A builder or other kind of contractor will be desirous of knowing the profit or loss he makes on each contract, and for that purpose keeps a separate account for each of them. The wages, materials, and other expenses will be charged against the contract in respect of which they have been incurred. Each contract will thus be kept as a distinct account, and the balance, whether debit or credit, will be transferred to the Profit and Loss Account.

Contracts. (margin)

Where the accounts are closed while contracts are in progress, the value of the work done on each contract will be calculated, and, after deducting any instalments received on account, the balances will appear in the Balance Sheet under " Contracts in Progress," in the list of assets.

Work in progress. (margin)

A paper given at one of the Society of Arts' examinations, which includes several contracts, is set out below :—

EXERCISE XII.

John Styles and Philip Brown, builders, had, on the 1st February 1887, respectively standing to their credit on Capital Account, £6,172 4s. 5d. for Styles, and £5,540 6s. 8d. for Brown. The statement of their affairs at that date was as under:—

ASSETS.					LIABILITIES.				
		£	s	d			£	s	d
H. Jones		728	5	11	Bills Payable, Nos. 38 and 39 ..		564	10	6
W. Wyes		314	7	6	D. McVey		348	5	9
Box & Cox		251	13	4	E. Ball		436	15	0
Bills Receivable—Nos. 65, 66 ..		748	10	6					
Contracts in Progress:—									
No. 17. Expenditure thereon £5,099 19 7									
Less instalments received 4,650 0 0									
		449	19	7					
No 18. Expenditure thereon 1,425 6 6									
Less instalments received 1,000 0 0									
		425	6	6					
No 19. Expenditure thereon 2,488 12 0									
Less instalments received 1,800 0 0									
		688	12	0					
Stock-in-trade		4,956	5	8					
Cash at Bank		827	11	4					
Machinery and Plant		3,615	0	0					
Cash in Office		56	10	0					

Each partner is credited monthly with interest at 5 per cent. on his capital, and the profits or losses are then divided equally.

Write up the various books and prepare Trial Balance Profit and Loss Account, and a Balance Sheet.

Their transactions for the month were as follows :—

All receipts and payments are made through the bank, except where *cash* is mentioned.

1887.						
Feb.	1.	Bought of D. McVey, Peterhead, Granite			£187 8 5	
,,	2.	Drawn from bank :—				
		Wages, Contract No. 17	£75 16 0			
		Do. do. No. 18	36 14 0			
		Do. do. No. 19	51 10 6			
		Do. General.. ..	25 16 0			
					189 16 6	
,,	4.	Accepted D. McVey's Draft at two months			187 8 5	
,,	,,	Received Instalment on Contract No. 17			754 0 0	
,,	,,	Paid Fire Insurance on do. ..			4 10 0	
,,	5.	Materials and Cartage supplied on :—				
		Contract No. 18			132 7 6	
		Do., No. 19			241 7 6	
,,	6.	Received Instalment on Contract No. 19			350 0 0	
,,	7.	Paid Acceptance No. 38			350 0 0	
,,	9.	Received Payment of Bill No. 65 ..			438 0 0	
,,	,,	Drew Cheque for Wages :—				
		Contract No. 17	£86 4 0			
		Do. No. 19	32 17 0			
		Sundry Wages	19 10 8			
					138 11 8	

1887.						
Feb.	9	Completed Contract No. 18 and received Final Instalment		900	0	0
,,	12.	Working Expenses, paid Rates (cheque)		28	15	0
		Do. Salaries (cash)		31	10	0
,,	14.	Materials and Cartage to:—				
		Contract No. 17		432	0	0
		Do. No. 19		216	0	0
,,	16.	Received Payment of Bill No. 66 ..		310	10	6
,,	,,	Paid John Styles (drawings)		300	0	0
,,	,,	Drew Cheque for Wages :—				
		Contract No. 17 .. .. £31 6 0				
		Do. No. 19 .. .. 82 5 8				
		Sundry Wages 14 10 0				
				128	1	8
,,	18.	Received Cash, Sundry Sales		15	8	6
,,	,,	Paid E. Ball's Account		430	0	0
,,	,,	Discount allowed		6	15	0
,,	,,	Working Expenses, Rent of Yard ..		48	0	0
,,	,,	Paid Philip Brown (drawings)		300	0	0
,,	20.	Materials and Cartage :—				
		Contract No. 17 .. .. £124 0 0				
		Do. No. 19 . .. 314 5 8				
				438	5	8
,,	,,	Received Cheque, W. Wyes		310	0	0
,,	,,	Discount allowed him		4	7	6
,,	,,	Received of Box & Cox, Final Dividend 17s. 6d. in the £		220	4	2
,,	23.	Wages, Contract No. 17		74	15	3
		Do. No. 19		52	4	0
,,	,,	Bought of Shaw & Co., Bricks as per invoice		215	0	0
,,	25.	Completed Contract No. 17, and received Final Instalment		1,000	0	0
,,	26.	Working Expenses, Cash for Sundries ..		21	13	0
,,	,,	Received Cheque, H. Jones		500	0	0
,,	28.	Credit John Styles Interest on Capital ..		25	13	4
,,	,,	Do. P. Brown do. ..		23	1	8
,,	,,	Paid Sundry Wages, Cash		31	7	6
,,	,,	Stock in hand		3,027	7	9
,,	,,	Wear and Tear of Plant		31	10	0

When we speak of balancing the accounts, we refer to the final closing when the Profit and Loss Account is being prepared at the end of a financial period, and the balances of the open accounts are brought down. Before balancing is attempted, attention should be given to the following suggestions :—

Balancing the Accounts

1. See that all the transactions are properly entered.
2. Examine to see if everything has been posted into the Ledger.
3. Check each Ledger Account to see if the balance we are taking out is the correct one.

If on taking out the Trial Balance the totals do not agree, we must proceed to find out the difference by discovering where the error has been made. We must feel perfectly satisfied in the first place that our work has been done correctly ; that for every debit we have a credit, and that the debit and credit postings in our Ledger accord with the entries made in the Cash Book or Journal. A check on these lines will soon enable us to balance the accounts, and achieve the purpose of double entry bookkeeping.

The author from his experience in teaching classes finds a word of advice to students necessary. The exercises, which are to be worked from week to week, should be diligently studied, and not after being gone through once be subsequently disregarded. Each exercise contains some special feature, and it is hoped that the variety of exercises selected will be of the greatest advantage to the student.

Glossary of Commercial Terms.

Abatement.—An allowance or sum deducted from an account.

Accommodation Bill.—A bill of exchange to which a person is a party, either as drawer, acceptor, or indorser, for which he has received no consideration, but done merely to accommodate another person.

Account Current.—A statement of account sent to a debtor at different periods showing balance owing by him.

Account Sales.—An account giving particulars of realisation of goods sold on commission, and charges payable on same.

Ad valorem Duty.—Duty charged on goods according to their *value*, and not on the quantity or weight.

Affreightment, Contract of.—A contract which contains an agreement for the carriage of goods in vessels for a price called " freight."

Affidavit.—A written statement verified on oath or affirmation, and signed by the person making it.

Average, Particular.—Damage done to the property of an individual by accident or otherwise, when not suffered for the general benefit, falls on the individual owner. No extraordinary compensation is granted in respect of such damage.

Average, General.—Where a certain portion of a ship's cargo has been sacrificed for the preservation of the ship and remaining cargo, the loss must be borne proportionately by all who are interested, or who have benefited by the sacrifice.

Bailment.—A delivery of goods in trust, which, when the trusts have been duly executed according to the contract, the goods shall be re-delivered. The person who receives the goods is called the bailee, the person who delivers them the bailor.

Bank Rate.—The rate of discount fixed by the Bank of England for discounting bills.

Barratry.—A wrongful act committed by the master or crew with intent to defraud the owner or the charterer of a ship.

Bill of Entry.—A printed list of goods received at the Custom House.

Bills of Lading.—A document acknowledging the shipment of goods, and containing the terms and conditions upon which it has been agreed that they are to be carried.

Bills of Sale.—An assignment of personal goods, giving a title to them without delivery, and executed in accordance with the Bills of Sale Act 1882.

Bottomry Bond.—A written instrument by which the master of a vessel raises money on the ship or its cargo, and in which he undertakes to repay the money on his safe arrival at home. It is a condition of such bond that if the vessel does not arrive at home the money is not repayable.

Capital of a Company.—Nominally the amount of capital stated in its memorandum of association, registered at Somerset House, London. A company is not entitled to receive more capital than the amount authorised in the aforesaid memorandum.

Caveat Emptor = (Let the buyer beware).—A maxim applied where goods are sold without any guarantee from the seller as to quality, &c.

Champerty.—A bargain made with a plaintiff or defendant to divide land or other matter sued for between them if they prevail at law, whereupon the champertee is to carry on the party's suit at his own expense.

Charter-Party.—A written agreement between a shipowner and another person or persons to place at their disposal an entire ship or part of it for conveyance of goods to a particular place for a sum of money, which the merchant undertakes to pay as freight for their carriage.

Contract Note.—A note sent by a broker or agent to his principal notifying him of the sale or purchase of any stock or marketable security.

Cumulative Preference Shares.—The same as preference shares, except that the dividend on these shares when not paid annually cumulates from year to year. Pending payment of dividend to holders of this class of shares, no dividend can be paid on ordinary shares.

Debentures.—Loans to public companies, generally on security of their assets, at a fixed rate of interest, repayable on expiration of term for which the amounts were lent. Interest on debentures is payable in priority to any other charges.

Del credere Commission.—An extra commission paid to an agent in consideration of his guaranteeing his principal against any losses from the sale of goods to persons introduced by him.

Demurrage.—An additional payment for detention of a vessel, whilst loading or unloading, beyond the period specified in the charter-party.

Document of Title.—A document used in the ordinary course of business as proof of the right to possession of the goods named therein.

Factor.—An agent to whom goods are consigned or delivered to be sold for his principal for an agreed commission. He is distinguished from a broker by (1) being able to sell in his own name, (2) to give a warranty, (3) to receive payment and give valid receipts, and other powers and privileges which are denied to a broker.

E

Flotsam.—Goods that float on the sea when the ship is sunk or otherwise perishes.

Goodwill.—The value of a business arising from the connection established between a firm and its customers.

Guarantee.—An agreement to be responsible for the debt, default, or miscarriage of another person.

Hypothecation.—The pledge of a vessel or its cargo as security for an advance of money.

Jetsam or Jettison.—Terms applied to the throwing of goods into the sea to lighten a ship when it is in danger of being sunk, and afterwards the ship perishes.

Lay Days.—The days named in a charter-party during which the vessel is allowed to load and unload its cargo.

Letters of Credit.—An authority addressed to a correspondent authorising him to pay the bearer of the letter a sum therein named.

Letter of Indemnity.—Protection given to a shipowner who delivers goods to a consignee who requires delivery before production of his document of title. Such letter when given is generally signed by a banker.

Lien.—There are various kinds of lien, but generally it pertains to a person who has possession of goods belonging to another, his lien entitling him to retain them until the debt due to him has been paid.

Mortgage.—A conveyance of land or property as security for the payment of money.

Mortgage Debenture Stock.—The same as debentures, except that the sums for which debenture stock is issued are not repayable by the company. On the winding-up of a company the holders of debenture stock are entitled to be paid, in full, the principal and interest due to them before any payment is made to creditors or shareholders of the company.

Ordinary Share Capital.—The capital of a company is usually divided into two classes, preference shares and ordinary shares. Where there is only one class, the whole is described as ordinary share capital. The holders of ordinary shares are entitled to receive the balance of profit earned by a company *after* payment of interest to debenture and preference shareholders. On the division of a company's assets the holders of ordinary shares rank last in order of precedence.

Paid-up Capital.—The amount actually paid up on the shares allotted to subscribers.

Preference Shares.—A part of the capital of a company, the holders of which receive a fixed rate of dividend on the amount paid up on their shares. In order of priority they come *after* debentures and *before* ordinary shares.

Rebate.—An allowance to an acceptor of a bill on payment of same before the due date. Deduction on account of prompt payment.

Recognisance.—An obligation imposed on a person in default.

Respondentia Bond.—A bond given where the cargo alone is hypothecated, although the term bottomry bond is often used in these cases.

Salvage.—The reward given to persons who save a ship, cargo, &c., from shipwreck or loss.

Set-off.—The right of one party who is bound under a contract towards another to set off a corresponding liability upon the side of that other party, as counterbalancing the want of performance of the contract sued upon.

Stoppage in transitu.—A right conferred on the unpaid seller who has parted with goods to stop them, on insolvency of the buyer, before they have reached the buyer's possession.

Subscribed Capital.—The nominal amount allotted to shareholders.

E 2

Usance.—The time which by usage or custom is allowed in certain countries for the payment of a bill of exchange.

Warranty.—An agreement collateral to a contract, the breach of which gives rise to a claim for damages, but not to reject the goods.

C.I.F.—Charges, insurance, freight.

F.O.B.—Free on board.

F.P.A.—Free of particular average.

C.F.I.—Cost, freight, and insurance.

EXAMINATION PAPERS

IN

BOOKKEEPING.

Society of Arts' Examination Paper 1888, fully worked by the Author.

As most students sitting for the Society of Arts' Examination generally find the time allowed for working the paper insufficient, they are, for examination purposes only, recommended to open as few subsidiary accounts as possible, and, if found advisable, to open only a Trading Account and Profit and Loss Account. The expenses must then be charged direct to the Profit and Loss Account, and the balance of the Trading Account will be transferred to Profit and Loss Account, as explained in previous chapters.

The Exercise.

Society of Arts' Examination Paper.

John Cross and Henry Pike carry on business as iron-founders in partnership, having £5,964 10s. 6d. and £3,724 15s. respectively standing to their credit on Capital Account on January 1st 1888.

Each is entitled to 5 per cent. interest on his capital, and the net profits or losses are then equally divided.

The following is the statement of their affairs at the beginning, and of their transactions during the month, of January. These you are required to write up in the proper books of account, and post in proper technical language and form, and to draw out a Trial Balance, Profit and Loss Account, and Balance Sheet, showing their adjusted Capital Accounts, after carrying thereto the results of their trading :—

Their Trading Debts were to—				
Alton & Co.	..	..	..	£177 13 2
Ford & Son	..	..	..	89 15 6
W. Jones	..	..	..	59 5 7
Sundry Persons ..	..	..	..	86 10 9
Acceptances granted not yet matured :—				
No. 86	..	..	£39 7 6	
„ 87	..	..	72 10 0	
				111 17 6
Their Assets comprised—				
Cash in Bank	..	..	..	486 12 10
„ Office	..	..	..	35 15 8
Bills Receivable—				
No. 61	..	..	£50 12 6	
„ 62	..	..	172 3 9	
„ 63	..	..	28 17 4	
				251 13 7
Debts on Open Accounts—				
H. Bland	..	..	..	152 6 4
A. Black ..	..	..	..	235 9 1
Stokes & Co.	..	..	..	73 5 6
Sundry Persons ..	..	..	..	527 8 6
Plant and Fixed Machinery	..	..	..	4,127 5 0
Moveable Plant	..	..	..	1,395 16 6
Stock-in-trade	..	..	..	2,928 15 0

1888.

Jan.	2.	Sold A. Black, 150 tons Railway Chairs at 60s.	450	0	0
,,	,,	Received his Acceptance at two months	450	0	0
,,	3.	Paid Water Rate by cheque	12	17	6
,,	,,	Bought of Alton & Co., for Acceptance at two months, Pig Iron 50 tons, at 42s.	105	0	0
,,	5.	Bill Receivable, No. 61, duly honoured ..	50	12	6
,,	,,	Received Cash, sundry Sales	18	10	8
,,	7.	Completed and delivered W. Jones's Contract, 8 Girders, 15 tons 10 cwts., at 64s.	49	12	0
,,	,,	Paid Wages	27	15	0
,,	9.	Retired Bill, No. 87	71	1	0
,,	,,	Discount on same	1	9	0
,,	,,	Sold S. Green, for Cash, sundry small Castings, 5 cwts. 14lbs., at 12s. ..	3	1	6
,,	11.	Received Cheque, Stokes & Co. ..	70	0	0
,,	,,	Allowed them Discount	3	5	6
,,	12.	Paid Acceptance, No. 86	39	7	6
,,	,,	Drew cheque for Office Cash	40	0	0
,,	14.	Bought of S. Green, 2 tons Copper, at £65, for acceptance at one month ..	130	0	0
,,	,,	Paid Wages	24	1	9
,,	16.	Paid Rates and Taxes, Cash	15	9	6
,,	,,	Received Cash, sundry Sales	21	11	6
,,	18.	John Cross, Capital drawn out ..	250	0	0
,,	,,	Sold Henry Norris, for Bill at two months, 12 Girders, 18 tons 10 cwts., at 60s.	55	10	0
,,	20.	Paid sundry Accounts, as per Cash Book, by cheques	74	1	5
,,	,,	Sold for Cash, 12 tons Castings, at 62s...	37	4	0
,,	21.	Paid Wages	21	10	0
,,	,,	Received Cash, sundry Sales	51	14	0
,,	23.	Bill No. 62, H. Norris, due this day, returned dishonoured	172	3	9
,,	,,	Paid Noting Charges		1	6
,,	24.	Cash sent to Bankers	60	0	0
,,	,,	Bought Foundry Sand for cash ..	4	10	0
,,	,,	Paid Alton & Co., Cheque	172	10	0
,,	,,	Discount allowed by them	5	3	2

1888.

Jan.	24.	Received of Trustee of H. Bland's Estate, first and final dividend of 10s. in the £	76	3	2
,,	26.	Sold Ford & Son, sundry Castings, 30 tons, at 60s.	90	0	0
,,	27.	Received of A. Black, on account ..	200	0	0
,,	,,	Received of H. Norris, amount of dishonoured Bill and Charges ..	172	5	3
,,	28.	Paid Wages	22	5	0
,,	,,	Received Cash Collections from sundry debtors as per Cash Book, and paid same into Bank	317	5	9
,,	30.	Henry Pike, Drawings	80	0	0
,,	,,	Sold S. Green, for Bill at three months, 70 Cast Columns, 31 tons 15 cwts., at 68s.	107	19	0
,,	31.	John Cross, Interest on Capital ..	24	17	8
,,	,,	Henry Pike, ,, ,, ..	15	16	0
,,	,,	Use and Wear of Stock and Machinery	17	10	0
,,	,,	,, ,, Movable Plant ..	8	7	6
,,	,,	Stock-in-trade, at cost price	2,736	15	9

EXAMINATION PAPERS.   59

THE EXERCISE.

Society of Arts' Examination Paper.

JOURNAL I.

1888 Jan. 1		Dr.		£ s d	£ s d
	Sundry Assets				
	To Sundry Liabilities				
	Cash in Office	Dr.	1	35 15 8	
	Cash at Bank	Dr.	1	486 12 10	
	Bills Receivable..	Dr.	11	251 13 7	
	H. Bland	Dr.	6	152 6 4	
	A. Black	Dr.	7	235 9 1	
	Stokes & Co.	Dr.	8	73 5 6	
	Sundry Debtors..	Dr.	9	527 8 6	
	Plant and Fixed Machinery ..	Dr.	13	4,127 5 0	
	Moveable Plant ..	Dr.	14	1,395 16 6	
	Stock-in-Trade ..	Dr.	17	2,928 15 0	
	To Alton & Co.		2	..	177 13 2
	„ Ford & Son		3	..	89 15 6
	„ W. Jones		1	..	59 5 7
	„ Sundry Creditors		5	..	86 10 9
	„ Bills Payable		12	..	111 17 6
	„ John Cross, Capital ..		23	..	5,964 10 6
	„ Henry Pike, do.		24	..	3,724 15 0
„ 2	A. Black	Dr.	7	450 0 0	
	To Sales Account ..		16	..	450 0 0
	150 tons Railway Chairs at 60/-				
„ „	Bill Receivable	Dr.	11	450 0 0	
	To A. Black..		7	..	450 0 0
	His acceptance at 2 months.				
„ 3	Purchase Account	Dr.	15	105 0 0	
	To Alton & Co.		2	..	105 0 0
	50 tons Pig Iron at 42/-				
„ „	Alton & Co.	Dr.	2	105 0 0	
	To Bill Payable		12	..	105 0 0
	Our acceptance at 2 months.				
„ 7	W. Jones ..	Dr.	1	49 12 0	
	To Sales Account ..		16	..	49 12 0
	15 tons 10 cwts. Girders at 64/-				
„ 14	Purchase Account	Dr.	15	130 0 0	
	To S. Green		4	..	130 0 0
	2 tons Copper at £65.				
„ „	S. Green	Dr.	4	130 0 0	
	To Bill Payable		12	..	130 0 0
	Our acceptance at 1 month.				
„ 18	Henry Norris	Dr.	10	55 10 0	
	To Sales Account ..		16	..	55 10 0
	18 tons 10 cwts. Girders at 60/-				
„ „	Bill Receivable ..	Dr.	11	55 10 0	
	To Henry Norris ..		10	..	55 10 0
	His acceptance at 2 months.				
„ 23	Henry Norris	Dr.	10	172 3 9	
	To Bill Receivable		11	..	172 3 9
	His acceptance returned dishonoured.				
	Carried forward			£ 11,917 3 9	11,917 3 9

JOURNAL—*continued*—II.

1888				£ s d	£ s d
Jan. 26	Brought forward	..	..	11,917 3 9	11,917 3 9
	Ford & Son	Dr.	3	90 0 0	
	To Sales Account		16	..	90 0 0
	30 tons Castings at 60/-				
" 30	S. Green	Dr.	4	107 19 0	
	To Sales Account		16	..	107 19 0
	31 tons 15 cwts. Cast Columns at 68/-				
" "	Bill Receivable	Dr.	11	107 19 0	
	To S. Green		4	..	107 19 0
	His acceptance at 3 months.				
" 31	Interest	Dr.	19	40 13 8	
	To John Cross, Drawings Account ..		25	..	24 17 8
	" Henry Pike, do. ..		26	..	15 16 0
	Interest on Capital.				
" "	Depreciation	Dr.	21	25 17 6	
	To Stock and Machinery		13	..	17 10 0
	" Moveable Plant		14	..	8 7 6
" "	Bad Debts	Dr.	22	76 3 2	
	To H. Bland..		6	..	76 3 2
	Balance of his debt written off.				
" "	Trading Account	Dr.	17	693 3 5	
	To Sundries				
	To Purchases		15	..	239 10 0
	" Wages		18	..	95 11 9
	" Depreciation		21	..	25 17 6
	" Profit and Loss		..	..	332 4 2
	For Balances transferred.				
" "	Sales	Dr.	16	885 2 8	
	To Trading Account		17	..	885 2 8
	For Balance transferred.				
" "	Profit and Loss	Dr.	27	332 4 2	
	To Sundries				
	To Interest and Discount		19	..	37 7 0
	" Rates and Taxes		20	..	27 17 0
	" Bad Debts		22	..	76 3 2
	" John Cross, Drawings A/c, half profit		25	..	95 8 6
	" Henry Pike, do. do.		26	..	95 8 6
	For Balances transferred.				
" "	John Cross, Drawings Account		25	120 6 2	
	To John Cross, Capital Account ..		23	..	120 6 2
	For Balance transferred.				
" "	Henry Pike, Drawings Account ..		26	31 4 6	
	To Henry Pike, Capital Account ..		24	..	31 4 6
	For Balance transferred.				
			£	14,427 17 0	14,427 17 0

SOCIETY OF ARTS' EXAMINATION 1888.

CASH.

1888	Particulars	Fol.	Discount £ s d	Cash £ s d	Bank £ s d
Jan. 1	To Balance at this date	1	..	35 15 8	486 12 10
" 5	" Bill Receivable	11	..		50 12 6
" "	" Sales A/c, Sundry Sales	16	..	18 10 8	
" 9	" do.	16	..	3 1 6	
" 11	" Do., Stokes & Co., Cheque £70 and Discount £3, 5s. 6d.	8	3 5 6		70 0 0
" 12	" Bank	✓	..	40 0 0	
" 16	" Sales A/c, Sundry Sales	16	..	21 11 6	
" 20	" Sales A/c, 12 tons Castings at 62s.	16	..	37 4 0	
" 21	" Sales A/c. Sundry Sales	16 ✓	..	51 14 0	
" 24	" Cash	6	..		60 0 0
" "	" H. Bland, Dividend of 10s. in the £	7 ✓	..		76 3 0
" 27	" A. Black	10	..		200 0 0
" "	" H. Morris, Amount of Bill and Charges	10	..		172 5 3
" 28	" Sundry Debtors	9	..		317 5 9
			£3 5 6	207 17 4	1,432 19 6
" 31	To Balance brought down		..	127 17 10	597 18 10

CONTRA.

1888	Particulars	Fol.	Discount £ s d	Cash £ s d	Bank £ s d
Jan. 3	By Rent, &c., Water Rate	20	..	..	12 7 6
" 7	" Wages	18	..	..	27 15 0
" 9	" Bill Payable, Retired	12	1 9 0	..	71 1 0
" 12	" Bill Payable, Paid Acceptance	✓	..	..	39 7 6
" "	" Cash	18	..	..	40 0 1
" 14	" Wages	20	..	..	24 1 9
" 16	" Rent, Rates and Taxes	23	..	..	
" 18	" John Cross, Capital A/c		..	..	
" 20	" Sundry Creditors, per Cheques		..	15 9 6	250 0 0
" 21	" Wages	18	..	..	74 1 5
" 23	" H. Morris, Noting Expenses	10 ✓	..	..	21 10 0
" 24	" Bank	15	..	60 0 0	1 1 6
" "	" Purchase A/c, Sand	2	5 3 2	4 10 0	
" "	" Alton & Co.	18	..	..	
" 28	" Wages	26	..	..	172 10 0
" 30	" H. Pike, Drawings		..	..	22 5 0
" 31	" Balance carried down		..	127 17 10	80 0 0 597 18 10
			£6 12 2	207 17 4	1,432 19 6

TRIAL BALANCE.

Folio							£ s d	£ s d
1	W. Jones ..	..	..	..	..	..	..	9 13 7
3	Ford & Son	..	..	..	..	..	4 6	
5	Sundry Creditors	..	..	..	..	..		12 9 4
7	A. Black ..	..	..	..	..	..	35 9 1	
9	Sundry Debtors	..	..	..	..	..	210 2 9	
11	Bills Receivable	..	..	..	..	..	642 6 4	
12	Bills Payable	..	..	..	..	..	..	235 0 0
13	Plant and Fixed Machinery ..	..	..	..	..	..	4,109 15 0	
14	Moveable Plant..	..	..	..	..	..	1,387 9 0	
15	Purchases	..	..	..	..	..	239 10 0	
16	Sales	..	..	..	..	..		885 2 8
17	Stock-in-Trade, 1st January..	..	..	..	..	2,928 15 0	
18	Wages	..	..	..	..	..	95 11 9	
19	Interest and Discount..	..	..	..	..	37 7 0	
20	Rent, Rates, and Taxes	..	..	..	..	27 17 0	
21	Depreciation	..	..	..	..	..	25 17 6	
22	Bad Debts	..	..	..	..	..	76 3 2	
23	John Cross, Capital	..	..	..	..	..		5,714 10 6
25	Do. Drawings..	..	..	..	..	..	24 17 8
24	Henry Pike, Capital ..	..	..	..	..	..	3,724 15 0
26	Do. Drawings	..	..	..	..	..	64 4 0	
C.B. 1	Cash in Office ..	..	..	..	..	..	127 17 10	
„ „	Cash at Bank ..	..	..	..	..	..	597 18 10	
							£10,606 8 9	£10,606 8 9

LEDGER ACCOUNTS.

Dr. (1)   W. JONES.   Cr.

1888				£ s d	1888				£ s d
Jan. 7	To Goods	..	1	49 12 0	Jan. 1	By Balance	..	1	59 5 7
„ 31	„ Balance	..	..	9 13 7					
				£59 5 7					£59 5 7
					„ 31	By Balance	..	..	9 13 7

Dr. (2)   ALTON & CO.   Cr.

				£ s d					£ s d
Jan. 3	To Bill Payable	1		105 0 0	Jan. 1	By Balance	..	1	177 13 2
„ 24	„ Cash and Discount	1		177 13 2	„ 3	„ Goods	..	1	105 0 0
				£282 13 2					£282 13 2

Dr. (3)   FORD & SON.   Cr.

				£ s d					£ s d
Jan. 26	To Goods	..	2	90 0 0	Jan. 1	By Balance	..	1	89 15 6
					„ 31	„ Balance	..	..	4 6
				£90 0 0					£90 0 0
„ 31	To Balance	..		4 6					

Dr. (4) S. GREEN. Cr.

			£ s d				£ s d
Jan. 14	To Bill Payable	1	130 0 0	Jan. 14	By Goods	1	130 0 0
„ 30	„ Goods	2	107 19 0	„ 30	„ Bill Receivable	2	107 19 0
			£237 19 0				£237 19 0

Dr. (5) SUNDRY CREDITORS. Cr.

			£ s d				£ s d
Jan. 20	To Cash	1	74 1 5	Jan. 1	By Balance	1	86 10 9
„ 31	„ Balance	..	12 9 4				
			£85 10 9				£86 10 9
				„ 31	By Balance		12 9 4

Dr. (6) H. BLAND. Cr.

1888			£ s d	1888			£ s d
Jan. 1	To Balance	1	152 6 4	Jan. 24	By Cash	1	76 3 2
				„ 31	„ Bad Debt	2	76 3 2
			£152 6 4				£152 6 4

Dr. (7) A. BLACK. Cr.

			£ s d				£ s d
Jan. 1	To Balance	1	235 9 1	Jan. 2	By Bill Receivable	1	450 0 0
„ 2	„ Goods	1	450 0 0	„ 27	„ Cash	1	200 0 0
				„ 31	„ Balance carried down	..	35 9 1
			£685 9 1				£685 9 1
„ 31	To Balance brought down	..	35 9 1				

Dr. (8) STOKES & CO. Cr.

			£ s d				£ s d
Jan. 1	To Balance	1	73 5 6	Jan. 11	By Cash and Discount	1	73 5 6

Dr. (9) SUNDRY DEBTORS. Cr.

			£ s d				£ s d
Jan. 1	To Balance	1	527 8 6	Jan. 28	By Cash	1	317 5 9
				„ 31	„ Balance carried down	..	210 2 9
			£527 8 6				£527 8 6
„ 31	To Balance brought down	..	210 2 9				

Dr. (10)   H. NORRIS.   Cr.

			£ s d				£ s d
Jan. 18	To Goods ..	1	55 10 0	Jan. 18	By Bill Receivable ..	1	55 10 0
" 23	" Bill Receivable ..	1	172 3 9	" 27	" Cash ..	1	172 5 3
" "	" Cash ..	1	1 6				
			£227 15 3				£227 15 3

Dr. (11)   BILLS RECEIVABLE.   Cr.

1888			£ s d	1888			£ s d
Jan. 1	To Balance ..	1	251 13 7	Jan. 23	By Henry Norris	1	172 3 9
" 2	" A. Black ..	1	450 0 0	" 5	" Cash ..	1	50 12 6
" 18	" H. Norris ..	1	55 10 0	" 31	" Balance carried down	..	642 6 4
" 30	" S. Green ..	2	107 19 0				
			£865 2 7				£865 2 7
" 31	To Balance brought down ..	..	642 6 4				

Dr. (12)   BILLS PAYABLE.   Cr.

			£ s d				£ s d
Jan. 9	To Cash and Discount	1	72 10 0	Jan. 1	By Balance ..	1	111 17 6
" 12	" Do.	1	39 7 6	" 3	" Alton & Co.	1	105 0 0
" 31	" Balance carried down	..	235 0 0	" 14	" S. Green ..	1	130 0 0
			£346 17 6				£346 17 6
				" 31	By Balance ..	..	235 0 0

Dr. (13)   PLANT AND FIXED MACHINERY.   Cr.

			£ s d				£ s d
Jan. 1	To Balance ..	1	4,127 5 0	Jan. 31	By Depreciation	2	17 10 0
				" "	" Balance carried down	..	4,109 15 0
		£	4,127 5 0			£	4,127 5 0
" 31	To Balance brought down ..	..	4,109 15 0				

Dr. (14)   MOVEABLE PLANT.   Cr.

			£ s d				£ s d
Jan. 1	To Balance ..	1	1,395 16 6	Jan. 31	By Depreciation	2	8 7 6
				" "	" Balance carried down	..	1,387 9 0
		£	1,395 16 6			£	1,395 16 6
" 31	To Balance brought down ..	..	1,387 9 0				

Dr. (15) PURCHASES ACCOUNT. Cr.

1888			£	s	d	1888			£	s	d
Jan. 3	To Alton & Co.	1	105	0	0	Jan. 31	By Trading Account	2	239	10	0
„ 14	„ S. Green ..	1	130	0	0						
„ 24	„ Cash ..	1	4	10	0						
			£239	10	0				£239	10	0

Dr. (16) SALES ACCOUNT. Cr.

			£	s	d					£	s	d
Jan. 31	To Trading Account ..	2	885	2	8	Jan. 2	By A. Black ..	1		450	0	0
						„ 7	„ W. Jones ..	1		49	12	0
						„ 18	„ H. Norris ..	1		55	10	0
						„ 26	„ Ford & Son	2		90	0	0
						„ 30	„ S. Green ..	2		107	19	0
						„ 5	„ Cash ..	1		18	10	8
						„ 9	„ Do. ..	1		3	1	6
						„ 16	„ Do. ..	1		21	11	6
						„ 20	„ Do. ..	1		37	4	c
						„ 21	„ Do. ..	1		51	14	0
			£885	2	8					£885	2	8

Dr. (17) MANUFACTURING AND TRADING ACCOUNT. Cr.

			£	s	d				£	s	d
Jan. 1	To Stock on hand ..	1	2,928	15	0	Jan. 31	By Sales ..	2	885	2	8
„ 31	„ Purchases..	2	239	10	0	„ „	„ Stock on hand ..	..	2,736	15	9
„ „	„ Wages ..	2	95	11	9						
„ „	„ Depreciation	2	25	17	6						
„ „	„ Profit and Loss ..	2	332	4	2						
			£ 3,621	18	5				£ 3,621	18	5
„ 31	To Stock-in-Trade ..	..	2,736	15	9						

Dr. (18) WAGES ACCOUNT. Cr.

			£	s	d				£	s	d
Jan. 7	To Cash ..	1	27	15	0	Jan. 31	By Trading Account ..	2	95	11	9
„ 14	„ Do. ..	1	24	1	9						
„ 21	„ Do. ..	1	21	10	0						
„ 28	„ Do. ..	1	22	5	0						
			£95	11	9				£95	11	9

Dr. (19) INTEREST AND DISCOUNT ACCOUNT. Cr.

			£	s	d				£	s	d
Jan. 31	To Sundries ..	2	40	13	8	Jan. 31	By Discounts per C.B...	1	6	12	2
„ „	„ Discounts per C.B...	1	3	5	6	„ „	„ Profit & Loss Account..	2	37	7	0
			£43	19	2				£43	19	2

F

Dr. (20)   RENT, RATES AND TAXES.   **Cr.**

				£ s d				£ s d
Jan. 3	To Cash	..	1	12 7 6	Jan. 31	By Profit & Loss		27 17 0
„ 16	„ Do.	..	1	15 9 6		Account..	2	
				£27 17 0				£27 17 0

Dr. (21)   DEPRECIATION ACCOUNT.   **Cr.**

			£ s d				£ s d
Jan. 31	To Sundries ..	2	25 17 6	Jan. 31	By Trading Account ..	2	25 17 6

Dr. (22)   BAD DEBTS ACCOUNT.   **Cr.**

			£ s d				£ s d
Jan. 31	To H. Bland ..	2	76 3 2	Jan. 31	By Profit & Loss Account..	2	76 3 2

Dr. (23)   JOHN CROSS, CAPITAL.   **Cr.**

				£ s d					£ s d
1888					1888				
Jan. 18	To Cash	..	1	250 0 0	Jan. 1	By Balance ..		1	5,964 10 6
„ 31	„ Balance	..	..	5,834 16 8	„ 31	„ Drawings Account ..		2	120 6 2
				£ 6,084 16 8					£ 6,084 16 8
					„ „	By Balance ..		..	5,834 16 8

Dr. (24)   HENRY PIKE, CAPITAL.   **Cr.**

							£ s d
			Jan. 1	By Balance ..	1		3,724 15 0
			„ 31	„ Drawings Account ..	2		31 4 6
						£	3,755 19 6

Dr. (25)   JOHN CROSS, DRAWINGS.   **Cr.**

			£ s d				£ s d
Jan. 31	To Capital Account ..	2	120 6 2	Jan. 31	By Interest ..	2	24 17 8
				„ „	„ Profit, half share ..	2	95 8 6
			£120 6 2				£120 6 2

Dr. (26)   HENRY PIKE, DRAWINGS.   Cr.

			£	s	d				£	s	d
Jan. 30	To Cash ..	1	80	0	0	Jan. 31	By Interest ..	2	15	16	0
„ 31	„ Capital Account ..	2	31	4	6	„ „	„ Profit, half share ..	2	95	8	6
			£111	4	6				£111	4	6

Dr. (27)   PROFIT AND LOSS ACCOUNT.   Cr.

1888			£	s	d	1888			£	s	d
Jan. 31	To Interest and Discount	2	37	7	0	Jan. 31	By Trading Account, gross profit ..	2	332	4	2
„ „	„ Rates and Taxes ..	2	27	17	0						
„ „	„ Bad Debts..	2	76	3	2						
			141	7	2						
„ „	„ John Cross, half share net profit	2	95	8	6						
„ „	„ Henry Pike, half share net profit	2	95	8	6						
			£332	4	2				£332	4	2

BALANCE SHEET, 31st January 1888.

Liabilities.	£	s	d	Assets.	£	s	d
Sundry Creditors :—				Cash in office ..£127 17 10			
On Open Account :—				Cash at Bank .. 597 18 10			
W. Jones ..£9 13 7					725	16	8
Sundry Accounts 12 9 4				Sundry Debtors :—			
	22	2	11	On Open Account :—			
On Bills Payable	235	0	0	Ford & Son .. 4 6			
John Cross, Capital	5,834	16	8	A. Black .. 35 9 1			
Henry Pike, Do.	3,755	19	6	Sundry Accounts 210 2 9			
					245	16	4
				On Bills Receivable ..	642	6	4
				Plant and Machinery ..	4,109	15	0
				Moveable Plant	1,387	9	0
				Stock-in-Trade	2,736	15	9
	£9,847	19	1		£9,847	19	1

EXERCISE I.

By the College of Preceptors.

1.—Write up the Cash Book, make necessary Journal entries, prepare Trial Balance, Profit and Loss Account and Balance Sheet.

June	1.	Cash in hand	£82 10 0		
,,	,,	Cash in .Union Bank ..	275 0 0		
,,	,,	Goods valued at	925 0 0		
,,	,,	C. Beaumont owes me ..	57 10 0		
			——£1,340 0 0		
,,	,,	I owe Graham & Co.	145 0 0	
,,	2.	Sold P. Stanley, Goods	37 12 6	
,,	,,	Bought of Graham & Co., Goods	175 15 0	
,,	,,	Sold for Cash, Goods	59 14 0	
,,	10.	Received from C. Beaumont, Cash ..	40 0 0	
,,	,,	Sold W. Russell, Goods	45 10 0	
,,	,,	Paid Graham & Co., Cash.. £100 0 0		
		And was allowed as Discount	5 0 0	
			105 0 0	
,,	,,	Sold Goods for Cheque, paid in Union Bank	56 0 0	
,,	15.	Sold for Cash, Goods	66 5 0	
,,	,,	Bought for Cash, Goods	73 15 0	
,,	,,	Sold C. Beaumont, Goods	48 2 6	
,,	,,	P. Stanley has paid into my Bank Account	25 12 6	
,,	20.	Paid Rates and Taxes	- 17 10 0	
,,	,,	Sold W. Russell, Goods	52 10 0	
,,	,,	Received from W. Russell, Cash £70 0 0		
		And I have allowed him as Discount	1 15 0	
			71 15 0	
,,	24.	Paid into Bank	60 0 0	
,,	,,	Paid Graham & Co., a Cheque on Union Bank for £150 0 0		
		And was allowed as Discount	7 10 0	
			157 10 0	
,,	,,	Paid Rent of Business Premises, by Cheque on Union Bank..	50 0 0	
,,	30.	P. Stanley has become insolvent and pays 8s. in the £, and I have received for his debt	4 16 0	
,,	,,	Paid Wages this month	12 10 0	
,,	,,	Estimated value of Goods unsold ..	875 0 0	

EXERCISE II.

By the College of Preceptors.

1.—Write up the Cash Book, make necessary Journal entries, prepare Trial Balance, Profit and Loss Account and Balance Sheet of the Imperial Coal Co., Limited, from the following transactions :—

			£	s	d
Jan. 1.	Capital at Bank		£10,000	0	0
,, 9.	Purchase from Clay, Cross & Co., 3,000 tons at 15s.		2,250	0	0
,, 11.	Purchase from Butterly Co., 2,000 tons at 14s.		1,400	0	0
,, 19.	Purchase from Cannock Chase Co., 500 tons at 12s.		300	0	0
,, 23.	Purchase Premises, and pay by Cheque		2,500	0	0
,, 29.	Pay by Cheque for Fitting up Premises		278	11	0
,, 31.	Paid by Cheque for Preliminary Expenses		450	9	0
Feb. 4.	Forwarded to Clay, Cross & Co., Acceptance at 2 months		1,000	0	0
	And Draft on Bank for		1,250	0	0
,, 11.	Sell to H. Clarke & Co., 1,650 tons at 16s. 6d.		1,361	5	0
,, 17.	Draw from Bank		200	0	0
,, 20.	Forward to Butterly & Co., a Cheque on Bank for..		1,200	0	0
Mar. 9.	Sell to MacBean & Co., 1,250 tons at 17s. 6d.		1,093	15	0
,, 11.	H. Clarke & Co. forward their Acceptance at 1 month for		1,000	0	0
,, 31.	Pay Salaries and other Expenses ..		85	0	0
April 5.	Forward to Cannock Chase Co., Cheque		200	0	0
,, 7.	The Bank pay Acceptance due to-day for		1,000	0	0
,, 12.	MacBean & Co. forward a Cheque ..		893	15	0
	And Acceptance at three months ..		100	0	0
,, 14.	H. Clarke & Co's. Acceptance duly honoured		1,000	0	0
,, 30.	Sell to Fitzwilliam & Co., 650 tons at 19s. 6d.		633	15	0
May 11.	Sell for Cash, 120 tons at 18s. 6d. ..		111	0	0
,, 24.	Fitzwilliam & Co. forward Cheque ..		633	15	0
,, 31.	Purchase from Cannock Chase Co., 620 tons at 14s. 6d...		449	10	0
,, ,,	Lodge in Bank		1,400	0	0
June 30.	Paid Salaries and other Expenses ..		64	9	3
,, ,,	Took Stock for Half-year, value on hand		2,700	0	0

EXERCISE III.

By the College of Preceptors.

1.—Write up the Cash Book, make necessary Journal entries, prepare Trial Balance, Profit and Loss Account and Balance Sheet from the transactions of Harry Clarke, as under :—

June	1.	Cash in hand	..	..	£39	10	0		
,,	,,	Cash at Bank	..	..	275	0	0		
,,	,,	Goods valued at	..	..	350	0	0		
,,	,,	T. Allen owes me	..	..	35	10	0		
								£700 0 0	
,,	,,	I owe Bennett & Co.	..	..	..			57 10 0	
,,	5.	Sold A. Carter, Goods	..	..	..			30 16 0	
,,	,,	Sold T. Allen, Goods	..	..	..			45 12 0	
,,	,,	Sold for Cash, Goods	..	..	..			37 7 6	
,,	10.	Received from A. Carter, Cash	..	..	..	£30	0	0	
		And I have allowed his Discount	..	..		16	0		
								30 16 0	
,,	12.	T. Allen has paid into my Bank Account						50 0 0	
,,	,,	Bought for Cash, Goods	..	..	..			67 10 0	
,,	,,	Sold A. Carter, Goods	..	..	..			24 15 0	
,,	,,	Sold W. Freeman, Goods	..	..	..			48 5 0	
,,	15.	Bought of Bennett & Co., Goods	..	..				56 16 0	
,,	,,	Paid Bennett & Co. a Cheque for	..	..	£100	0	0		
		And was allowed by them a Discount of	..	..		5	0	0	
								105 0 0	
,,	,,	Received from W. Freeman, Cash	..					40 0 0	
,,	20.	Sold for Cash, Goods	..	..	..			36 12 6	
,,	29.	W. Freeman has become insolvent, and I have received for his debt a dividend of 10s. in the £	..	..	..	..		4 2 6	
,,	,,	Paid Rent of Warehouse, by Cheque	..					20 0 0	
,,	,,	Paid into Bank, Cash	..	..	..			75 0 0	
,,	30.	Paid Trade Expenses during the month						7 17 6	
,,	,,	Estimated value of Goods unsold is	..					300 0 0	

EXERCISE IV.

By the College of Preceptors.

1.—Write up the Cash Book, make necessary Journal entries, prepare Trial Balance, Profit and Loss Account and Balance Sheet, showing position of affairs of S. Blinker on 31st May :—

April	1.	I have in hand Cash ..	£35 0 0			
,,	,,	In Bank	365 0 0			
,,	,,	Goods valued at	250 0 0			
,,	,,	T. Ashton owes me.. ..	45 0 0			
				£695	0	0
,,	,,	I owe Mapleson & Co.		72	10	0
,,	10.	Sold to R. Oakley, Goods		65	15	0
,,	,,	Bought of Mapleson & Co., Goods ..		127	10	0
,,	,,	Sold to T. Bircham, Goods		56	5	0
,,	30.	Sold Goods for Cash this month		92	12	6
May	4.	Received from R. Oakley, Cash	£50 0 0			
		And I have allowed him a Discount of	1 5 0			
				51	5	0
,,	,,	Bought Goods for Cash		75	0	0
,,	,,	Sold to T. Ashton, Goods		67	10	0
,,	15.	Paid Mapleson & Co. a Cheque for	£150 0 0			
		And they have allowed me a Discount of	7 10 0			
				157	10	0
,,	,,	C. Bircham paid to my Bank Account ..		50	0	0
,,	,,	Bought Goods for Cheque..		84	16	0
,,	24.	Received from J. Ashton, Cash		48	0	0
		And his Acceptance at 3 months for ..		50	0	0
,,	,,	Sold Goods for Cheque and sent it to Bank		33	10	0
,,	,,	Paid into Bank, Cash		100	0	0
,,	30.	Paid Cash for Warehouse Repairs ..		15	0	0
,,	,,	Paid Clerk's Salary by Cheque on County Bank		26	5	0
,,	,,	T. Bircham having failed, I received for his debt a dividend of 8s. in the £ ..		2	10	0
,,	31.	Sold Goods for Cash this month ..		87	15	0
..	..	Estimated value of Goods unsold ..		225	0	0

Exercise V.

By the College of Preceptors.

1.—Write up the Cash Book, make necessary Journal entries, prepare Trial Balance, Profit and Loss Account and Balance Sheet.

Carter & Co. commence the year under the following conditions :—

Jan.	1.	They owe to R. Thomas £1,560	0 0
,,	,,	R. Brown owes them 420	0 0
,,	,,	They hold Merrion & Co.'s Bill in their favour for 300	0 0
,,	,,	Goods in hand, valued at 750	0 0
,,	,,	Cash in hand 2,000	0 0
,,	,,	Cash in Bank 1,000	0 0
,,	2.	Forward to Bank the above Bill for collection 300	0 0
,,	3.	Purchase from Simmons & Co., Goods .. 1,233	10 0
,,	4.	Pay Simmons & Co.—By Cash 77	0 0
		By Cheque .. 500	0 0
		By Bill, due Jan. 28, for 650	0 0
		By Discount allowed 6	10 0
,,	,,	Lodge in Bank 1,200	0 0
,,	8.	Forward to R. Thomas, Cheque 5E0	0 0
,,	,,	And Acceptance at 3 months 1,000	0 0
,,	11.	R. Brown pays to Bank 400	0 0
,,	18.	Sell to R. Brown, Goods 260	10 0
,,	,,	Sell to S. Lush, Goods 170	0 0
,,	,,	Sell for Cash, Goods 36	10 0
,,	20.	R. Brown forwards me his Acceptance for 150	0 0
,,	21.	S. Lush settles his Account, Cash .. 168	0 0
,,	,,	Discount 2	10 0
,,	23.	Sell to Baker Bros., Goods.. 978	10 0
,,	,,	Sell to R. Brown, Goods 338	10 0
,,	25.	Receive from Baker Bros. their Acceptance at 1 month 478	10 0
,,	26.	R. Brown forwards me Cash 169	0 0
,,	28.	The Bank honour my Acceptance to Simmons & Co. for 650	0 0
,,	31.	Paid Month's Expenses, by Cash.. .. 96	10 0
,,	,,	Paid Rent by Cheque 87	10 0
,,	,,	Goods on hand, valued at.. .. .. 4C0	0 0

EXERCISE VI.

Civil Service Examination Paper.

1.—Write up the Cash Book and Journal, and prepare Trial Balance, Profit and Loss Account, and Balance Sheet.

The following are balances brought down in J. Grey's Ledger, on December 31st:—

			Dr.			Cr.		
Jan.	1.	John Smith	£115	2	9			
,,	,,	W. Faber	31	5	6			
,,	,,	Bank	490	9	8			
,,	,,	J. H. Jones	7	11	2			
,,	,,	Goods..	75	10	0			
,,	,,	W. W. Cooper & Co. ..				£465	4	0
,,	,,	Capital				222	10	0
,,	,,	Bills Receivable ..	38	7	2			
,,	,,	Bill Payable				192	16	8
,,	,,	Cash	122	4	5			
,,	4.	Bought of W. W. Cooper & Co., Goods				315	0	0
,,	,,	Faber's Acceptance due this day, paid at Bank ..				38	7	2
,,	,,	Sold W. Moffett, Goods ..				154	5	6
,,	10.	Received of W. Faber, his Acceptance at 1 month ..				31	5	6
,,	,,	Received of W. Moffett ..				154	5	6
,,	,,	Paid W. W. Cooper & Co., by Cheque	315	0	0			
		Less 7½ per cent... ..	22	13	0			
						291	7	0
,,	15.	Paid into Bank				250	0	0
,,	,,	Accepted Draft of W. W. Cooper & Co. at 3 months				465	4	0
,,	,,	Drew Cheque for Private Personal Expenses ..				50	0	0
,,	,,	Bought of Johnson & Co., Goods				105	17	2
,,	17.	Sold J. Doubleday, Goods ..				11	15	9
,,	21.	Sold R. Jameson, Goods ..				115	5	4
,,	24.	J. & J. Smith's Draft, due this day, paid at Bank ..	122	16	8			
,,	,,	John Smith paid into my Bank Account	105	2	9			
		Less Discount	2	17	9			
						112	5	0
,,	28.	J. H. Jones absconded bankrupt ; his debt a total loss				7	11	2
,,	31.	Wrote off as provision for future Bad Debts ..				25	0	0
,,	,,	Petty Expenses paid during month				17	11	0
,,	,,	Rent still due to J. Smart..				10	0	0

EXERCISE VII.

Civil Service Examination Paper.

On the 31st December 1884, A. Aubret starts business with a capital of £3,000 in cash at the Bank of London.

On the 1st January 1885, he purchases the business, with the assets, stock, and liabilities of J. Blackham, for which he pays £2,500.

The Balance Sheet of J. Blackham, on the 31st December 1884, stood as follows :—

	£ s d		£ s d
To Goods	1,500 0 0	By National Bank	53 8 10
„ Bills Receivable	250 0 0	„ Bills Payable	184 3 2
„ T. Williams	294 8 6	„ D. Wilkinson	30 18 5
„ C. Anthony ..	305 11 6	„ Capital	2,081 9 7
	£2,350 0 0		£2,350 0 0

The Waste Book of A. Aubret contains the following transactions :—

1885.

			£ s d
Jan.	2.	Consigned to A. Fernandez, of Oporto, per steamship *Walrus*, on his account and risk, Goods valued at	£800 0 0
„	„	Freight and Dock Charges on the above shipment	15 6 10
„	3.	Bought of T. Joyce, Goods..	123 18 0
„	„	Bought of C. Twist, Goods	82 5 4
„	5.	Received of T. Williams, in part payment of his debt to J. Blackham, his Cheque	150 0 0
„	„	Allowed T. Williams for Discount ..	2 18 6
„	10.	J. Blackham's acceptance to T. Moore, paid this day by cheque	150 0 0
„	12.	Accepted draft of T. Joyce, at 1 month	123 18 0
„	13.	Paid into Bank	100 0 0
„	20.	Bought of S. Wortley, Goods	172 17 6
„	„	Accepted Bill of S. Wortley for	172 17 6
„	27.	Paid Cash for freight on consignment ..	12 2 4
„	31.	Paid Clerk's Salary due this day	10 0 0

1885.

Feb.	1.	Bought of C. Twist, Goods	302	18	6
,,	,,	Bought of T. Soper, Goods	93	16	2
,,	7.	Sold T. Joyce, Goods	422	3	4
,,	,,	Paid Carriage of same	1	18	6
,,	12.	Drew Bill on C. Anthony in respect of his debt to J. Blackham	305	11	6
,,	15.	My acceptance to T. Joyce, paid at Bank	123	18	0
,,	20.	Discounted with Samuel & Co., C. Anthony's Bill, and received their cheque on the London and County Bank	303	10	0
,,	,,	Allowed Discount	2	1	6
,,	25.	Accepted C. Twist's Draft at 1 month	300	0	0
,,	,,	Paid C. Twist, by cheque	83	0	0
,,	,,	Discount allowed by C. Twist	2	3	10
,,	26.	Received of A. Fernandez a cheque on the London and County Bank for £450, on account of my consignment to him ..	450	0	0
,,	28.	Charged T. Williams interest upon the balance of his debt to J. Blackham..	1	5	0
,,	,,	Paid for Petty Office Expenses	3	2	1

Write up Cash Book and Journal, post all the transactions into the Ledger, inserting the proper folio references.

Balance and close the Ledger, showing the Trial Balance, Profit and Loss Account, and Balance Sheet.

Goods on hand valued at £917 17s. 2d.

EXERCISE VIII.

Society of Arts' Examination Paper.

Write up, and post in proper technical language and form, the following transactions, and make out from the Ledger a Trial Balance, a Profit and Loss Account, and a Balance Sheet :—

On the 1st January 1882, John Rose, Cooper, was possessed of the following business assets :—

Freehold Premises, valued at				£3,000	0	0
Plant and Machinery				1,608	0	0
Stock-in-trade				2,410	19	2
Office Furniture..				106	5	0
Cash at Bankers	£915	1	6			
and in Office	16	5	9			
				931	7	3
Bills receivable :—						
Ship Brewery Co., due Jan. 7 ..	231	6	6			
R. Conway, due Jan. 19 .. .	174	10	0			
J. Smith, due March 6	88	11	8			
				494	8	2
Book Debts :—						
F. Stamp	251	3	8			
C. Hart	113	5	0			
				364	8	8
				8,915	8	3
At the same time he owed :—						
On Bills Payable :—						
S. Hill, due Jan. 4	186	0	0			
P. Jones, due Jan. 12	219	0	0			
				405	0	0
To Creditors :—						
N. Hobbs	376	18	0			
Stiff & Co.	527	3	7			
				904	1	7
				1,309	1	7

His transactions for the month were :—

Jan.	1.	Paid Stiff & Co. their account, less 2½ per cent. for cash		514	0	0
,,	,,	Sold Star Brewery Co., for net cash, 150 kildns., at 14s.		105	0	0
,,	3.	Received of F. Stamp .. £245	0 0			
,,	,,	Allowed him discount .. 6	3 8			
				251	3	6
,,	,,	Paid Fire Insurance		57	13	0
,,	4	Paid S. Hill's draft, due this day ..		186	0	0
,,	5.	Paid Office Expenses for week		10	5	6
,,	,,	Wages as per Wages Book		74	8	9

Jan.	7.	Received payment of Ship Brewery Co.'s acceptance		231 6 6	
,,	9.	Bought of Stiff & Co., Timber, per invoice		357 11 6	
,,	11.	Drew cheque for Office Cash		30 0 0	
,,	12.	Bought Hoop Iron of N. Hobbs, 3 tons, at £15 10s.		46 10 0	
,,	,,	Paid Office Expenses for week		11 15 0	
,,	,,	Paid Wages		82 19 0	
,,	,,	Paid P. Jones's bill, due this day ..		219 0 0	
,,	14.	Sold W. Stroud & Co.:—			
		100 barrels at 21s. 6d. ..	£107 10 0		
		200 kildns. at 13s. 9d. ..	137 10 0		
,,	,,	Drew on them for amount at 2 months:		245 10 0	
Jan.	16.	Paid Repairs to Boundary Wall		14 15 6	
,,	,,	Paid for Portable Steam Engine, delivered this day, per contract with W. Edleston	£120 0 0		
		Less 5 per cent., as agreed..	6 0 0		
				114 0 0	
,,	18.	Paid Poor and Highway Rates		27 15 9	
,,	19.	R. Conway's acceptance dishonoured ..		174 10 0	
,,	20.	Paid Office Expenses		13 17 6	
,,	,,	Paid Wages		79 5 10	
,,	,,	Sold Trueman & Co. 750 casks, at 21s.	£787 10 0		
		Less 5 per cent.	39 7 6		
				748 2 6	
,,	,,	Drew on them at 2 months for		500 0 0	
,,	,,	Received Cash to balance		248 2 6	
,,	22.	Paid N. Hobbs		150 0 0	
,,	,,	Received payment of R. Conway's dishonoured bill and expenses		174 11 6	
,,	23.	Sold for Cash to W. Stroud & Co.—			
		350 barrels at 20s. ..	£350 0 0		
		Less 5 per cent. discount ..	17 10 0		
				332 10 0	
,,	24.	Received first and final dividend of 3s. in the £ on debt owing by C. Hart ..		16 19 9	
,,	,,	Paid Subscription to Hospital		21 0 0	
,,	,,	Paid Water Rate		15 17 6	
,,	26	Bought for Cash of P. Loader, Coal, 40 tons at 12s. 6d.		25 0 0	
,,	,,	Paid Gas Company's Bill		36 15 10	
,,	,,	Drew Cheque for Office Expenses ..		25 0 0	
,,	27.	Sold H. Joyce (net) :—			
		200 hogsheads at 25s. ..	£250 0 0		
		150 kilderkins at 14s. ..	105 0 0		
				355 0 0	
,,	,,	Received Cash		200 0 0	
,,	,,	Received Acceptance, due 30th March ..		155 0 0	
,,	,,	Paid Office Expenses for week		9 1 6	
,,	,,	Paid Wages, as per Wages Book		67 14 0	
,,	31.	Paid Midland Railway Carriage Account for month..		27 19 0	
,,	,,	Stock of Goods on hand		2,122 17 0	

EXERCISE IX.

City of London College Paper.

A.—James Key and William Read commence business in partnership on the 1st January, agreeing to divide profits equally.   At the end of the year they value their stock-in-trade at £1,000, and produce the following Trial Balance.   Prepare Balance Sheet and Profit and Loss Account, showing the state of their affairs at 31st December.

James Key, Capital Account	..	.. ..	£1,000 0 0
William Read, Capital Account	..	.. ..	1,000 0 0
Sales	..	.. ..	6,500 0 0
Cash	.. £300 0 0		
Bills Receivable	.. 750 0 0		
Bills Payable	..		200 0 0
A. Brand	..		42 10 0
T. Keating	.. 63 10 0		
D. Lambert	.. 228 10 0		
G. Welch	.. 95 0 0		
W. Clarke	.. 608 0 0		
R. Carter	..		25 10 0
S. Harris	.. 338 0 0		
Bad Debts	.. 83 0 0		
Purchases	.. 5,000 0 0		
Rent, Salaries, and other Charges	.. 492 0 0		
James Key, Drawings ..	.. 388 0 0		
William Read, Drawings ..	.. 422 0 0		
	£8,768 0 0		£8,768 0 0

B.—Lambert, Welch and Clarke are in partnership, and have at credit of their respective Capital Accounts on the 1st January £3,000, £2,500, and £2,000.   The partnership deed provides that each partner is to receive interest at 5 per cent. per annum on his capital, and that the profits are to be divided in the proportions—one-half, one-third, and one-sixth.   After·

deducting interest, the net profit on the year's trading was £1,700, and the partners' drawings were respectively £900, £600, and £500. Make up the partners' accounts so as to show the final Balances at the 31st December.

C.—Write up the Cash Book and Journal from the following transactions:—

Jan. 1. You buy 100 tons of Coal from George Washington, at 15s. per ton, delivered.

" 5. You give George Washington your Promissory Note at 3 months for £75.

" 6. You sell 80 tons of Coal to John Adams at 17s. per ton.

" 10. John Adams gives you his Acceptance to your draft at 3 months for £68.

" 21. You discount the £68 acceptance at your bankers, who credit your Current Account with £67 7s. 6d. in respect thereof.

" 22. You pay sundry charges for £15 by cheque on your bankers.

" 24. You buy 200 tons of Coal from George Washington, at 15s per ton.

" 28. You give George Washington your Promissory Note at 3 months for £150.

Feb. 3. You sell 150 tons of Coal to Thomas Jefferson, at 16s. 9d. per ton.

" 7. You receive from Thomas Jefferson his Acceptance to your draft at 1 month for £125 12s. 6d., which you discount at your bankers on the same day for £125 2s., placed to credit of your Current Account.

April 8. Your Promissory Note due this day is paid by your bankers.

" 12. Adams's Acceptance is retired, he giving you a new one at 1 month for £68 7s., which you discount immediately, getting credit at your bankers for £68 1s.

D.—Show the following Ledger Accounts as posted from your entries of the transactions above recorded:—

John Adams,

Bankers' Current Account,

and state what amount of profit you would have made—if any.

EXERCISE X.

Examination for County of Lancaster Commercial Exhibitions to Evening Classes, 1892.

On June 30 1892 the books of Allen & Co. were closed with the following balances :—Cash in hand, £16 12s. 8d. ; Cash at bank, £138 12s. 4d. ; Stock of goods, £1,500 ; Business Premises, £1,200 ; Bills Receivable, £723 18s. 10d. ; Bills payable, £329 2s. 9d. ; Sundry debtors, viz. :—T. Davis, £83 3s. 8d. ; Mackenzie Brothers, £109 13s. 4d. ; Sundry creditor, viz. :—Wood & Co., £113 13s. 8d.

N.B.—Cash in hand is to be kept distinct from cash at the bank. All cheques pass through the bank the same day.

The following are the transactions of July :—

July	2.	Bought Goods from Wood & Co. ..		£76	14 3
,,	3.	Our acceptance, No. 13, due to-day, paid by Bank		143	13 4
,,	4.	Discounted with Bank the following Bills—			
		No. 19, Roberts & Co. ..	£125 4 7		
		No. 20, James Phillips..	203 3 2		
			328 7 9		
		Discount ..	1 7 1		
				327	0 8
,,	6.	Sold Goods to T. Davis		84	4 3
,,	7.	Amount of Watson & Co.'s acceptance, No. 17, due to-day, collected by Bank..		229	9 2
,,	8.	Our acceptance, No. 14, due to-day, paid by Bank		185	9 5
,,	11.	Paid to T. Davis, by order, and for account of Wood & Co. (cheque)		120	0 0
,,	13.	Bought Goods from Mackenzie Brothers..		74	4 8
,,	14.	Paid Mackenzie Brothers in full settlement of Invoice of Goods bought yesterday (cheque)		72	0 0
,,	16.	Sold Goods to Davis & Co.		329	2 9
,,	17.	Amount of J. Richards' Acceptance, No. 8, due to-day, collected by Bank ..		166	1 11

July 18. Sold a portion of the Business Premises,
        receiving cheque for 400 0 0
        And invested the proceeds in Railway
        Shares costing 401 12 9
        Pay for same by cheque.

  ,, 21. Received from Mackenzie Brothers—
        Their Acceptance at
           1 m/d £75 0 0
           Cheque 25 0 0
           Cash 9 13 4
                                       109 13 4

  ,, 24. Sold Goods to Davis & Co. 74 12 10
  ,, 27. Received from Davis & Co. (cheque)   ..   100 0 0
        And their Acceptance at 1 m/d   ..   300 0 0
  ,, 31. Bank received Dividend on Railway
        Shares (to be included in month's profits)   7 10 0
  ,, ,, Paid Office Expenses for one month (Cash)   13 4 6

Write up the Cash Book, journalise the transactions, post
the Ledger, take out the Trial Balance, close the books,
making the necessary Journal entries, and draw up a Balance
Account. Take goods on hand as worth £1,200.

Exercise XI.

City of London College Paper.

On the 1st January 1882 John Atkins, previously a clerk in an underwriter's office, and whose assets consisted of £2,000 Consols, worth in cash £2,060, a house and land called Tithebarn Place, valued at £4,000 (there being no liabilities), commenced business as insurance broker and underwriter.

He arranged with Ezekiel Abrahams & Co., merchants, that he should have all their orders for insurances, taking his brokerage on the premiums, and giving them the benefit of the discount at 10 per cent., which underwriters allow for monthly payments, and that their partners, Jonas Abrahams and Eli Moss, should employ him to underwrite in their names, each paying him £150 per annum certain, and one-third of the profits derived from their underwriting, after payments of all losses and expenses, including interest at 5 per cent. on the capital they might provide him with in relation to such underwriting. In case of loss, one-third thereof, similarly ascertained, to be borne by John Atkins.

All cash, save petty cash, is understood to pass through the Banking Account.

1882.

Jan.	1.	Received from Union Bank, advance of £1,000 on security of £2,000 Consols, the said sum being placed to credit of a Current Account opened with that Bank.			
,,	,,	Drawn from Bank for petty cash	£50	0	0
,,	15.	Insured £6,000 on ship *Amethyst* at six guineas per cent., debited E. Abrahams & Co., insurance £378, and stamp £3	381	0	0
,,	,,	Credited sundry Underwriters for said Insurance	359	2	0
		And Brokerage	18	18	0

1882.

Jan. 31. Premiums underwritten this month for
sundry Brokers—

On account, Jonas Abrahams	..	78 15	6
On account, Eli Moss	..	77 19	0
On account, John Atkins	..	76 15	0

Feb. 10. Received from sundry Brokers for January
Premiums, less 10 per cent. discount ..   210 2 7

,, ,, Paid sundry Underwriters for Insurance
per *Amethyst* 323 3 10

,, ,, Allowed sundry Brokers Discount—

On account, Jonas Abrahams	..	7 17	6
On account, Eli Moss	..	7 15	11
On account, John Atkins	..	7 13	6

,, ,, Credited E. Abrahams & Co., Discount, deducted from sundry Underwriters' Accounts 35 18 2

,, ,, Cash received of E. Abrahams & Co.   ..   345 1 10

,, 25. Settled General Average with Underwriters
on ship *Amethyst* amounting to   ..   83 7 8

,, ,, And credited same to E. Abrahams & Co.
after deducting 1 per cent. brokerage,
say, 16s. 8d.

,, 28. Premiums underwritten this month :—

On account, Jonas Abrahams	..	94 14	9
On account, Eli Moss	..	93 11	6
On account, John Atkins	..	92 15	0

,, ,, Losses and Averages settled this month :—

On account, Jonas Abrahams	..	257 18	0
On account, Eli Moss	..	207 18	0
On account, John Atkins	..	157 18	0

,, ,, Returns settled this month :—

On account, Jonas Abrahams	..	4 15	0
On account, Eli Moss	..	4 15	0

And credited sundry Brokers accordingly.

Mar. 4. Received of Jonas Abrahams on account of
his underwriting capital 100 0 0

,, ,, Received similarly of Eli Moss 50 0 0

,, 10. Drawn from Bank for Petty Cash   ..   50 0 0

,, ,, Paid E. Abrahams & Co. 82 11 0

,, ,, Received of sundry Underwriters   ..   83 7 8

,, ,, Paid sundry Brokers 379 5 10

1882.

				£	s.	d.
Mar.	10.	Allowed sundry Brokers Discount :—				
		On account, Jonas Abrahams	..	0	0	
		On account, Eli Moss	.. ..	8	17	
		On account, John Atkins	.. ..	9	5	6
„	31.	It appears that of £100 drawn out for petty cash, £78 had been spent for salaries and office expenses, £3 for stamp, and there remained £19.				
„	„	Premiums underwritten this month :—				
		On account, Jonas Abrahams	..	181	19	0
		On account, Eli Moss	..	179	15	0
		On account, John Atkins	..	163	14	0
„	„	Averages settled this month :—				
		On account, Jonas Abrahams	..	28	16	3
		On account, Eli Moss	..	28	16	3
„	„	Returns settled this month :—				
		On account, Jonas Abrahams	..	4	2	6
		On account, Eli Moss	.. ..	4	2	6
		On account, John Atkins	.. ..	3	15	0

The discount of 10 per cent. on premiums less returns is to be credited to the brokers on the March business, and Jonas Abrahams and Eli Moss having been charged with the proper sums for three months' fixed charges, and interest having been computed on their capital to 31st March, £100 on each of the three underwriting accounts being carried forward as a provision for unascertained losses, the balance of the respective underwriting accounts is then to be adjusted as per agreement. Interest at 3 per cent. to 31st March is to be computed on the Union Bank Loan, and the exact position of John Atkins on 31st March thus ascertained.

EXERCISE XII.

Union of Lancashire and Cheshire Institute's Examination,
1892.

1.—Write up the Cash Book and Journal. Post into Ledger. Prepare Trial Balance, Profit and Loss Account, and Balance Sheet.

Assets.

Cash at Manchester and County Bank	£3,000	0 0
Bill Receivable—No. 8, J. Marsh, due 6th March..	1,350	0 0
C. Wolland owes	150	0 0
Sugar, valued at	1,520	0 0

Liabilities.

J. Wood, due to him	50	0 0
Bill Payable—No. 64, J. Shaw, due 31st March, accepted and payable at Bank	170	0 0

The interest of A. C. Brown in the above is £4,200, and he is to receive three-fourths of the profits, the remainder is to belong to David Wallace, who is to receive one-fourth of the profits and £250 per annum for salary. All cash and cheques are to be paid direct into the bank, and all payments are to be made by cheques on the bank. Capital and drawings to bear interest at 5 per cent. per annum.

In the succeeding five months their transactions were as follows :—

Jan. 1.	Bought of Simon Wilson, 50 casks Coffee	£1,700	0	0
,, ,,	Paid Simon Wilson by Cheque ..	1,700	0	0
,, 2.	Drew from Bank for Petty Cash ..	50	0	0
,, 10.	Received advice from Langworthy & Co., Hong Kong, of their purchase, on Joint Account with ourselves, of 200 chests Tea, which they intend shipping per *Queen Mary*	1,502	10	0
,, ,,	Insured on Tea, per *Queen Mary*, £1,500 at 70s. per cent. and stamp, with Thames and Mersey Marine Insurance Company..	52	13	9
,, 20.	C. Wolland, paid by Cheque his debt £150 0 0			
,, ,,	Interest on same.. .. 10 0	150	10	0

Jan.	25.	Accepted Langworthy & Co.'s draft (with Bill of Lading of Tea, per *Queen Mary*, attached), No. 47, at 3 months' date..	1,502	10	0
Feb.	5.	Sold to W. Law, 25 casks Coffee for ..	950	0	0
		And received his cheque for the amount.			
,,	8.	Paid Thames and Mersey Marine Insurance Company, by Cheque £52 13 9			
,,	,,	*Less* Commission allowed .. 5 5 9			
			47	8	0
,,	20.	Bought of S. Walls, for account of Winter & Co., Rotterdam, 1,500 bags of Sugar, and shipped per *Lion*	1,200	0	0
,,	,,	Due to S. Walls for brokerage	6	2	0
,,	,,	Manchester Ship Canal for shipping charges	16	5	0
,,	,,	For insurance on 1,500 bags of Sugar, say, £1,400 at 5 per cent., with Thames and Mersey Marine Insurance Co. ..	70	0	0
,,	,,	Our Commission	25	0	0
,.	,,	Paid S. Walls, by Cheque	1,226	2	0
Mar.	8.	Paid into Bank Bill Receivable, No. 8, due 6th March	1,350	0	0
,,	10.	Received from Winter & Co., Rotterdam, Bill Receivable, No. 9, at 3 m/d, on King, King & Co.	1,250	0	0
,,	31.	Manchester and County Bank paid Bill, No. 64, due this day	170	0	0
,,	,,	A. C. Brown drew from Bank	50	0	0
Apr.	23.	"*Queen Mary*" having arrived, we have retired our Acceptance, No. 47, with Bill of Lading	1,502	10	0
,,	30.	Paid freight on our Joint Account Tea, per "*Queen Mary*," by Cheque ..	95	0	0
,,	,,	Paid Landing Charges on same by Petty Cash	25	0	0
May	29.	Sold to Turner & Co., our 200 chests Joint Account Tea, and received their Cheque	1,890	0	0
,,	,,	Made up our account of our Joint Account Tea, and charged for Commission ..	35	0	0
,,	30.	Paid Rent of Office	75	0	0
,,	,,	Paid Clerks' Salaries	90	0	0
,,	,,	Paid Manchester Ship Canal Co. ..	16	5	0
,,	,,	A. C. Brown's interest on Drawings ..	8	4	
,,	,,	A. C. Brown's interest on Capital ..	87	10	0
,,	,,	David Wallace's interest on Capital ..	33	6	8
,,	,,	Value of Coffee on hand	940	0	0
,,	,,	Value of Sugar on hand	1,520	0	0

Exercise XIII.

Union of Lancashire and Cheshire Institutes' Examination,
1893.

Up to 31st December 1892, James Midwood carried on business as a wholesale wine and spirit merchant on his own account. In recognition of the faithful services of his traveller, David Brice, he decided to take him into partnership as and from 1st January 1893, Brice to bring in £1,000 capital, and to be entitled to one-third of the profits each year, the partnership to be carried on in the name or style of Midwood & Brice.

On the 1st January 1893 the books of James Midwood showed the position of his affairs to be as stated below :—

Assets : Cash at Bankers, £1,000 ; Cash in hand, £50 ; Port Wine, 5 pipes at £60, £300 ; Sherry, 6 butts at £50, £300 ; Dowley & Son, debt on open account, £450 ; Bills Receivable, No. 114, January 15th 1893, Wm. Bell & Co., £900 ; Total, £3,000. Liabilities, Hans Johnsen, £300 ; Thomas Buckley, £300 ; Bills Payable, No. 60, due January 12th 1893, J. Nooks, £500 ; Total, £1,100.

Each partner's capital is to be credited with interest at the rate of 5 per cent. per annum before arriving at the balance of profit and loss.

During the month of January the transactions of the firm were as follows :—

Jan.	1.	Brice paid into Bank Account of firm his portion of Capital £1,000		0	0
,,	2.	Sold to Dowley & Son, 3 pipes Port Wine for	210	0	0
,,	3.	Paid Cash for Dock Charges on 3 pipes Port sold yesterday	8	15	0
,,	5.	Bought 40 hhds. Brandy, at £40, from E. Lintott and gave him a Bill at 2 months, he allowing 2½ per cent. ..	1,600	0	0

Jan.	8.	Shipped per *Annie*, on Joint Account with ourselves and Harrison & Co., Liverpool, each one-half concerned, 40 hhds. Brandy, invoiced at £50	2,000	0	0
,,	,,	Received Debit Notes as below:—			
		Insurance on Brandy..	31	0	0
		Dock Charges ..	25	0	0
		Commission to Charles Kells & Co...	41	2	5
,,	12.	Paid Dock Company's Charges by Cheque	25	0	0
,,	,,	Bank advise having paid Bill No. 60 this day..	500	0	0
,,	,,	Received Cheque, crossed not negotiable, for £1,000, from Harrison & Co., being their half-share per *Annie*	1,000	0	0
,,	14.	Paid Anglo Assurance Company, by Cheque, £31 Insurance on £2,400, at 25 per cent., on Brandy, per *Annie*, for Sydney	31	0	0
,,	15.	William Bell & Co.'s Bill, No. 114, for £900, returned dishonoured	900	0	0
,,	,,	Paid Cash for Noting Charges ..		3	6
,,	,,	Sold W. Scott, 4 butts Sherry for	270	0	0
,,	,,	Received Cash £270, for Sherry sold to W. Scott, and paid to Bank	270	0	0
,,	,,	Paid Cash £11 12s., Dock Charges on Sherry sold to W. Scott..	11	12	0
,,	31.	Paid Trade Charges, £15, for expenses this month	15	0	0
,,	,,	Stock on hand—Port	125	0	0
,,	,,	Stock on hand—Sherry	110	0	0

EXERCISE XIV.

Union of Lancashire and Cheshire Institutes, 1897.

On the 1st January 1897, the books of Godfrey Simpson showed the position of his affairs to be as follows:—

Property and Assets:—

(a) Business Premises			£500 0 0
(b) Wine in stock and bond ..	.. £1,000 0 0		
Brandy ,, ,, ..	.: 1,000 0 0		
		2,000 0 0	
(c) J. Wall, Open Account		205 0 0	
(d) Bills Receivable, viz.:—			
J. South	.. £200 0 0		
T. North	.. 152 0 0		
		352 0 0	
(e) Cash in hand..		52 10 4	
(f) Cash in Union Bank of Manchester		553 2 0	
		3,662 12 4	

And Liabilities:—

(a) Bills Payable, viz.:—		
J. Sandbach & Sons	300 0 0	
(b) W. Brown, Open Account	44 0 0	
(c) Godfrey Simpson, Capital	3,318 12 4	
	3,662 12 4	

Requiring additional capital, David Scott was admitted into partnership as and from 1st January 1897. Scott introduced £2,000, which was paid to the credit of the partnership account at the Union Bank of Manchester on the 15th January 1897.

Each partner to draw £20 per month. Simpson to have two-thirds profit and Scott one-third.

Interest at the rate of 5 per cent. per annum to be allowed on the capital, and 5 per cent. per annum to be charged on drawings.

Business premises to be depreciated at the rate of 5 per cent. per annum.

1897.			
Jan.	2.	Bought additional Business Premises ..	£200 0 0
,,	,,	Discounted J. South's Acceptance ..	197 10 0
,,	,,	Discount	2 10 0
,,	6.	Bought Wine for Cheque	342 10 0

1897.						
Jan.	7.	Sold Brandy for Cheque	845	0	0
,,	9.	Bought Brandy from J. Black	400	0	0
,,	10.	Drew Cheque from Bank for loan to Jno.			
		South	100	0	0
,,	13.	Sold G. Green, Wine	500	0	0
,,	,,	Accepted G. Green's Bill, due March			
		16th 1897	300	0	0
,,	,,	G. Green accepted our Bill at 2 m/d ..	200	0	0
,,	15.	David Scott paid in his share of Capital			
		to the Union Bank	2,000	0	0
,,	,,	Received Cheque from J. Wall	200	0	0
		Allowed Discount	5	0	0
,,	16.	Paid W. Brown, Cash	40	0	0
		Discount allowed by him	2	0	0
,,	20.	Sold Brandy to J. Wilson	240	0	0
,,	,,	Sold J. Wilson, Wine	800	0	0
,,	,,	Received J. Wilson's Acceptance at 21 days	1,040	0	0
,,	30.	Bought schooner *Dolphin* from J. Wall	2,000	0	0
		And paid Cheque for charges for			
		bringing her from Newcastle to			
		Manchester	25	0	0
,,	,,	Paid Cash for repair to *Dolphin*	12	10	0
,,	,,	Paid Cheque to ;J. Wall, Account			
		Dolphin	1,000	0	0
,,	,,	Accepted J. Wall's draft at 2 m/d, being			
		balance of purchase money account of			
		Dolphin	1,000	0	0
,,	31.	Paid Trade Charges:—			
		Salaries to Clerks by Cheque	30	0	0
		Gas, Water, and Coal by Cheque ..	3	10	0
,,	,,	Private Drawings for the month, viz. :—			
		G. Simpson £32 0 0			
		D. Scott 20 0 0			
			52	0	0
,,	,,	L. and Y. Railway Co.'s Account for			
		carriage of wines and spirits during the			
		month	15	0	0
,,	,,	Effected an Insurance of Business			
		Premises and Stock for £2,000, and			
		paid premium at 5s. per cent.			
,,	,,	To accommodate Mort & Sons, accepted			
		J. Wallis's draft at 2 m/d for ..	100	0	0
		And charged them Commission and			
		Interest..	1	10	6
,,	,,	Allowed G. Green £20 for loss of Wine			
		through leakage	20	0	0
,,	,,	Paid Cooperage, by Cheque	2	10	6
,,	,,	Stock on hand, Wine	200	0	0
,,	,,	Stock on hand, Brandy	350	0	0

EXERCISE XV.

Scotch Leaving Certificate, 1896.

Charles Mitchell, having purchased the iron foundry business of J. Strachan & Co., Aberdeen, finds his assets and liabilities, at 1st January 1895, to be :—

Assets: Premises, £1,370 ; Manufactured Goods, £2,375 ; Pig Iron, £570 ; Sundry Goods (used in manufacturing), £335 ; Goodwill, £350 ; Town and County Bank, £4,500 ; Cash on hand, £50 ; Total, £9,550.

Liabilities: Capital, £4,550 ; J. Strachan & Co., £5,000 ; Total, £9,550.

He makes the following transactions :—

1895.

Jan.	1.	Paid J. Strachan & Co., to Account (by Cheque) £4,000	0	0
,,	2.	Cash lodged in Bank	30	0	0
,,	,,	Sold Ramsay & Taylor, Manufactured Goods, invoiced at	690	10	0
,,	4.	Sold A. Rutherford, Manufactured Goods, invoiced at	865	12	6
,,	20.	Purchased from J. Williamson & Co., Pig Iron, invoiced at	320	5	0
,,	31.	Purchased from William Crawford, Sundry Goods, invoiced at	125	6	8
Feb.	4.	Received from Ramsay & Taylor ..	621	9	0
,,	,,	Discount allowed them	69	1	0
,,	,,	Received from A. Rutherford, to Account	100	0	0
,,	,,	Above amounts received to-day, lodged in Bank	721	9	0
,,	15.	Sold Ramsay & Taylor, Manufactured Goods, invoiced at	422	7	6
,,	,,	Sold A. Rutherford, Manufactured Goods, invoiced at	270	2	6
,,	20.	Purchased from J. Williamson & Co. Pig Iron, invoiced at	210	3	0
,,	,,	Purchased from Wm. Crawford, Sundry Goods	62	7	0

1895.

Feb. 27.	Paid for Repairs to Premises (by Cheque)		23	9	6
,, 28.	Borrowed from A. Kinnaird, bearing interest at 5 per cent.		500	0	0
,, ,,	Same lodged in Bank		500	0	0
,, ,,	Paid John Williamson & Co.'s January Account (by Cheque)		288	4	6
,, ,,	Discount allowed by them..		32	0	6
Mar. 1.	Paid J. Strachan & Co. (by Cheque) ..		1,008	8	6
,, 3.	Paid Wm. Crawford his Account (by Cheque)		168	18	4
,, ,,	Discount allowed by him		18	15	4
,, 31.	Cheque drawn for Cash		250	0	0
,, ,,	Paid Wages (in Cash)		235	4	0
,, ,,	Paid Insurance (in Cash)		15	15	6

On the 31st March Charles Mitchell shows his goods on hand as follows :—Manufactured Goods, £1,341 3s. 8d.; Pig Iron, £490 3s.; Sundry Goods, £320 5s.

Frame Journal entries for the following :—March 1st, allow J. Strachan & Co. interest on £1,000 for 2 months at 5 per cent. (£8 6s. 8d.).

March 31st, allow for interest at 5 per cent. to A. Kinnaird, on £500 for 1 month, £2 1s. 8d.

Write £50 off goodwill. Write up the Cash Book and Journal.

Post all the entries to Ledger Accounts. Separate Ledger Accounts should be opened for each class of expenditure, viz., wages, insurance, &c.

Frame a Profit and Loss Account (or a Trading Account and a Profit and Loss Account), and carry the balance to the debit or credit of Charles Mitchell's Capital Account. Then frame a Balance Sheet.

Exercise XVI.

Society of Arts, 1895

William Stokes and John Wright, silk mercers, had respectively capital, on 1st January 1895, £2,126 15s. and £1,850 10s., and their liabilities on that date were :—

Bills Payable, No. 54	£178	10	0
Bills Payable, No. 55	220	14	6
Samuel Grice, Open Account	285	7	10
Philip Jones, Open Account	338	8	6
Heiros & Co., Open Account	468	13	10

Their assets at the same time were :—

Stock-in-trade, at cost price	2,648	11	9
Cash at Bankers	497	10	6
Cash in Warehouse	106	5	9
Bills in hand :—			
Holland & Joyce, No. 214	176	9	4
Smith & Co., No. 125	108	10	0
Broad & Hatton, No. 216	201	5	5
Lease of Warehouse, valued at	500	0	0
Fittings and Fixtures	124	0	0
Consignments in the hands of Giobo & Co., Cape-town, invoice prices	845	0	0
Book Debts :—			
William Robins	107	15	4
Holland & Joyce	56	17	0
King & Kerry	96	14	7

Their transactions for the month are set forth below. You are required to record and post these in proper technical language, and, having balanced the accounts, to draw out Trial Balance, Profit and Loss Account and Balance Sheet, with profits and losses divided equally (after crediting 5 per cent. interest on capital), and carried to the Partners' Capital Accounts.

All receipts are paid into the bank the same day, and all payments over £5, unless otherwise stated, are by cheque.

Jan.	2.	Sold Wm. Robins, Goods as per invoice..	£114	10	0
,,	4.	Paid Bill No. 55, due this day	220	14	6
,.	5.	Received from Giobo & Co., Account Sales of Consignment in their hands, net proceeds, with bill for that amount due Feb. 17	1,017	4	6
,.	,,	Received Cash, Sundry Sales	15	9	6
,	6.	Paid Cash, Water Rate	3	2	4
,,	7.	Received Payment, Bill No. 216	201	5	5
,,	,,	Paid Cash, Fire Insurance	2	14	6
,,	9.	Bought of Hieros & Co., Goods	194	15	0
		Gave them bill at 2 months ..	550	0	0
,,	11.	Bill No. 214 returned dishonoured ..	176	9	4
,.	,,	Paid noting		1	6
,,	12.	Paid Porters' and Messengers' Wages ..	4	7	6
,,	13.	Sold Broad & Hatton, Goods per invoice	84	9	6
,,	,,	Received Cash, Sundry Sales	27	14	9
,,	16.	Paid Bill No. 54, due this day	178	10	0
,,	,,	Paid Cash, Sundry Warehouse Charges ..	2	15	0
,,	18.	Received of Holland & Joyce, for Bill and Charges	176	10	10
,,	20.	Consigned to Giobo & Co., at our risk and account, Goods invoiced at	1,210	18	6
,,	,,	Paid Freight, Insurance, and Charges thereon	36	1	9
,,	21.	Bought of Philip Jones, Goods for bill at 2 months	489	9	6
,,	23.	Sold Wm. Robins, Goods as per invoice..	60	10	0
,,	,,	Paid Samuel Grice (discount £10 7s. 10d.)	275	0	0
,,	24.	Paid Cash, additional Warehouse Fittings	15	10	0
,,	,,	Received of William Robins, Cheque ..	130	0	0
,,	,,	Received of William Robins, Bill at 2 months	152	15	4
,,	26.	Drawn out by William Stokes	50	0	0
,,	,,	Drawn out by John Wright	50	0	0
,,	,,	Received of King & Kerry, first and final dividend, 15s.	72	10	11
,,	27.	Paid Cash, Porters' and Messengers' Wages	4	7	6
,,	,,	Sold Broad & Hatton, Goods as per invoice	241	9	8
		And received from them Cheque for	300	0	0 .

Jan.	28.	Received of Holland & Joyce	56	15	6
,,	,,	Received payment of Bill No. 215 ..	108	10	0
,,	31.	Paid Cash, Warehouse Salaries for mouth	17	14	0
,,	,,	Paid Cash, Postages and Parcels for month		16	3
,,	,,	Credited William Stokes, Interest on Capital	8	17	2
,,	,,	Credited John Wright, Interest on Capital	7	15	10
,,	,,	Stock on hand at this date	1,915	5	9
,,	,,	Depreciation of Fittings and Fixtures ..	3	1	6

EXERCISE XVII.

Society of Arts, 1890.

Henry Fox, iron merchant, at January 1st 1890 had a balance at his banker's of £1,724 10s., and cash in office £85 16s. 4d.

His bills in hand amounted to £704 7s. 6d., being Acceptances No. 74, £186 17s. 6d.; No. 76, £300; and No. 77, £217 10s.

Debts owing to him on open accounts were: By Joseph Ball, £58 19s.; Thomas King, £275 18s. 4d.; William Wright, £285 9s. 9d.; and Henry Dale, £178 10s.

He had also goods on consignment with Henry Poole, Smyrna, of the cost value of £680.

His freehold business premises were valued at that date at £1,740, and his stock-in-trade at £2,876 15s. He had given acceptances, which were then current, as follows: No. 43, £281 10s.; No. 44, £250; No. 45, £140 16s. 8d.

He owed on open accounts: To Sims & Co., £85 1s. 6d.; Jones & Young, £41 17s.; Percy Bright, £60; and John Kerr, £102 5s. 6d. Find and credit his capital.

On the same date he admitted as partner Joseph Crane, who paid into the Bank Account £3,000 as his capital, to receive, in accordance with the deed of partnership, one-fourth of the profits, Henry Fox guaranteeing the debts then owing to the concern, and reserving a preferential claim to the extent of £50 on the first month's profits in respect of business previously done.

The further transactions of Fox & Crane for the month of January are subjoined.

You are invited to arrange and post their accounts and draw out a Trial Balance, Profit and Loss Account, and Balance Sheet, with the results of their trading carried to their Capital Accounts.

All amounts for £5 or over were paid by cheque, all under that amount in cash, unless otherwise stated. All cheques received were paid into the bank the same day.

Jan.	2.	Bought of Sims & Co., for 4 months' bill, less 2½ per cent., 100 tons of Angles, at £8	£780	0	0
,,	3.	Paid them Cheque..	81	0	0
,,	,,	They allowed Discount	4	1	6
,,	,,	Sold Henry Dale, for prompt cash, less 2½ per cent., 20 tons Bars, at £9	175	10	0
,,	5.	Received payment of Bill No. 74 ..	186	17	6
,,	,,	Sold Hugh Forbes, for 2 months' bill, 12 tons Fish Plates, at £8..	96	0	0
,,	6.	Shipped on consignment to Henry Poole, Smyrna, 80 tons Angles, at £8.. ..	640	0	0
,,	,,	Paid Freight, Insurance, and Charges thereon	56	2	9
,,	,,	Debited Sims & Co., for short delivery Angles, 1 ton, 15 cwts., at cost.. ..	13	13	0
,,	,,	Paid Wages	4	5	0
,,	8.	Paid Fire Insurance on office and ware-house	3	5	0
,,	,,	Received payment Bill No. 77, due this day..	217	10	0
,,	10.	Sold on commission, at 2s. 6d. per ton, for the Western Steel Co., to Joseph Ball, 70 tons Steel Rails, at £7 per ton, on 3 months' acceptance	490	0	0
,,	,,	Endorsed and forwarded acceptance to Western Steel Co., debited them with commission	8	15	0
,,	12.	Bought of Percy Bright, 12 cwt. Rivets, at 22s.	13	4	0
,,	,,	Paid him	70	0	0
,,	,,	Discount allowed	3	4	0
,,	13.	Sold Hugh Forbes, 10 cwts. Rivets, at 25s. 6d. for net cash for 1 month ..	12	15	0
,,	,,	Paid Wages	4	5	0
,,	15.	Received of Henry Poole, Smyrna, Account Sales and sight draft.. ..	750	6	8
,,	,,	Received of William Wright, Cheque ..	280	0	0

H

Jan. 16.	Paid John Kerr	100	0	0
,,	,,	Discount allowed by him	2	5	6
,,	17.	Paid Water Rate	2	12	6
,,	,,	Received Western Steel Co.'s Cheque for commission	8	15	0
,,	18.	Retired under discount acceptance given to Sims & Co., 2nd inst., for	768	10	0
,,	19.	Sold William Wright, for 3 months' bill, 100 tons Bars, at £8 10s. net	850	0	0
,,	20.	Paid Wages	4	5	0
,,	22.	Bought of Western Steel Co., 40 tons Steel Sleepers, at £7 10s.	300	0	0
,,	,,	Paid Cheque, less 2½ per cent. allowed ..	292	10	0
,,	23.	Paid Poor Rates	5	3	4
,,	25.	Paid Acceptance, due this day, No. 43 ..	281	10	0
,,	,,	Received of Henry Dale, Cheque on account	150	0	0
,,	26.	Paid Jones & Young	40	15	0
,,	,,	Discount allowed	1	2	0
,,	27.	Received of Trustee of Thomas King, first and final dividend of 19s. in the £	262	2	5
,,	,,	Debited loss hereon to Henry Fox's separate account..	13	15	11
,,	,,	Paid Wages	4	5	0
,,	29.	Received Account Sales, Sight Draft, and Stock Account from Henry Poole, Smyrna, Consignment	420	0	0
,,	30,	Paid Plumber's Account, warehouse roof..	2	1	9
,,	,,	Paid Acceptance No. 44, due this day ..	250	0	0
,,	,,	Received Cash, sundry small sales ..	9	15	0
,,	31.	Paid Clerk's Salary	12	10	0
,,	,,	Debited Depreciation of Premises and Furniture..	5	0	0
,,	,,	Value of Stock on hand—cost price ..	2,346	7	4
,,	,,	Value of Stock on consignment, Smyrna	338	4	6
,,	,,	Petty Expenses paid for month	4	13	8
,,	,,	Credited Henry Fox, Rent of warehouse and office	10	0	0

EXERCISE XVIII.

Society of Arts' Examinations.—Second Examination, 1896.

The following was the statement of affairs of Arthur Archer, wine merchant, on 31st January 1896 :—

Liabilities.	£	s	d	Assets.	£	s	d
Bills Payable — No. 241,				Stock in hand, in cellars,			
£187 16s. ; No. 242, £150..	337	16	0	and with agents, at cost :.	3,070	15	0
Overdraft at Bankers ..	213	5	0	Bills Receivable—No. 104,			
Concia & Co., Lisbon ..	824	17	6	£137; No. 105, £50 ..	187	0	0
Druitt & Duse ..	596	10	0	Stock on consignment with			
Sundry Creditors	1,438	10	9	Henry Hart, Montreal ..	874	10	6
A. Archer's Capital	4,364	2	6	Europa Club	185	6	0
				Grant & Green	72	15	0
				Sundry Debtors :—			
				Agents	1,144	9	6
				Trade Accounts	2,240	5	9
	£7,775	1	9		£7,775	1	9

On February 1st the business was transferred to Bruce Balfour on the following terms :—The capital, together with a premium of £800 for goodwill, to be paid on taking possession, in cash £1,664 2s. 6d., and three promissory notes for £1,000, £1,000, and £1,500 at 3, 4, and 6 months, any of which might be retired at any time, less a rebate at 6 per cent., Balfour taking all the assets, with all profits and risks, and undertaking to discharge all liabilities.

You are required to open accounts for these particulars, to record and post the following transactions of Bruce Balfour, to balance the accounts, and finally to prepare a Trial Balance, Profit and Loss Account, and Balance Sheet. All receipts paid into bank the same day, and all payments, unless otherwise stated, by cheque.

1896.

Feb. 1. Paid Cash into Bankers £3,000 0 0

,, ,, Delivered to Arthur Archer, Cheque .. 1,664 2 6

,, ,, Delivered to Arthur Archer, 3 Promissory
Notes, Nos. 243, 244, and 245 for £1,000,
£1,000, and £1,500 .. .. .. 3,500 0 0

1896.

			£	s.	d.
Feb.	1.	Drew Cheque for office cash	50	0	0
,,	3.	Drew Bill, No. 106, at 3 months on Europa Club, which they accepted ..	150	0	0
,,	,,	Sold Kirk & Co., Wines, as per invoice ..	72	10	0
,,	4.	Received Cash, sundry trade debtors collected, as per Cash Book	238	0	0
,,	7.	Paid Traveller's Commission and Expenses	14	0	0
,,	,,	Sold Kirk & Co., 10 cases Champagne ..	38	10	0
,,	10.	Accepted Concia & Co.'s Bill at 3 months	700	0	0
,,	,,	Paid them Cheque	124	17	6
,,	12.	Received from Henry Hart Account Sales of consignment, with sight draft net proceeds	936	17	6
,,	15.	Paid Local Board Rates	8	1	4
,,	,,	Paid Law Costs, Transfer of Business ..	23	6	8
,,	18.	Received Payment of Bill No. 104 ..	137	0	0
,,	,,	Sold Lord Lingrove, Wines as per invoice	185	0	0
,,	19.	Received of Kirk & Co., Cash	109	0	0
		Allowed them Discount..	2	0	0
,,	,,	Shipped on consignment to Henry Hart, Wines at cost	742	0	0
,,	,,	Paid Shipping Charges, Freight and Insurance..	13	12	6
,,	21.	Sold Europa Club, 10 cases Claret at 15s.	22	10	0
,,	25.	Paid off Bill No. 245, under rebate ..	1,461	0	10
,,	,,	Accepted Druitt & Duse's draft at 3 months	500	0	0
,,	28.	Paid Bookkeeper and Month's Wages, office cash	28	9	4
Mar.	1.	Received of Henry Hart on account consignment	450	0	0
,,	,,	Received of sundry agents Cash as per Cash Book	284	0	0
,,	3.	Bought of Nuelli & Co., 10 pipes Port for bill at 4 months	580	0	0
,,	5.	Sold sundry Wines, as per Day Book ..	421	5	0
,,	7.	Paid sundry Trade Creditors, as per Cash Book	356	10	0
,,	9.	Received of Ochoa & Co., Wines on consignment	746	15	0
,,	,,	Paid Dock Charges	5	9	6

1896.

Mar.	12.	Roso's Bill, No. 105, returned dishonoured and noting	50	1	6
,,	,,	Drew Cheque for office cash	20	0	0
,,	15.	Sold Lord Lingrove, further Wine ..	81	15	0
,,	17.	First and final dividend, 17s. 6d. in the £, from Grant & Green	63	13	2
,,	18.	Sold out of Bond goods consigned by Ochoa & Co.	825	0	0
,,	,,	Charged Commission 5 per cent... ..	41	5	0
,,	,,	Remitted them 7 days' draft in settlement	778	5	6
,,	20.	Bought of Druitt & Duse, 40 cases Champagne	120	0	0
,,	22.	Paid Bill No. 241	187	16	0
,,	,,	Received Cash, sundry agents ..	203	5	0
,,	,,	Received Cash from R. Rose for bill and expenses	50	1	6
,,	24.	Sold Europa Club, for cash, Wines ..	39	15	0
,,	,,	Received Cash, sundry trade accounts ..	234	7	4
,,	26.	Bought of Nuelli & Co., Claret	78	10	0
,,	,,	Claimed on them for ullage (leakage) of Port, claim allowed	5	0	0
,,	,,	Paid them Cheque	69	11	6
,,	,,	Discount allowed	3	18	6
,,	30.	Paid Month's Wages and Petty Expenses, office cash..	29	6	6
	31.	Paid Quarter's Rent, offices and cellars..	25	0	0
,,	,,	Stock-in-Trade, valued at cost	2,341	4	6

EXERCISE XIX.

Society of Arts' Examination, 1894.

The following shows the state of affairs of Messrs. John and Joseph Tough, ironwork contractors, at January 1st 1894, followed by a record of their transactions during the month.

You are required to arrange and post these transactions to proper accounts opened in the Ledger, and having balanced them to draw out a Profit and Loss Account, Trial Balance, and Balance Sheet, to credit each partner with 5 per cent. interest on his capital, and carry the amount of the profit or loss in equal shares to their respective Capital Accounts.

All payments over £5 by cheque, unless otherwise stated; all under that amount in coin; all receipts paid into bank same day.

Liabilities.—Capital: John Tough, £13,057 14s. 1d.; Joseph Tough, £15,960 1s. 6d. Sundry Creditors: Peter Jones, £923; John Smith, £1,027 16s.; Henry Brown, £450. Bills payable, No. 391, £1,000; No. 392, £850 10s. Instalments received on Current Contracts: No.124, Wessex Bridge, £960; No. 125, Mercia Tanks, £1,845; No. 126, Cantia derricks, £2,460. Mortgage on Premises, £15,000. *Assets.*— Freehold Works valued at £26,000; Plant, Machinery and Rolling Stock, £5,280; Cash at bankers, £2,456 1s. 9d.; Cash in office, £84 7s. 4d.; Bill receivable, No. 248, £365. Sundry Debtors—Value of work done: No. 124, Wessex Bridge, £1,530 2s. 9d.; No. 125, Mercia Tanks, £3,160 10s. 4d.; No. 126, Cantia derricks, £5,130 12s. 8d.: No. 127, Devonia Viaduct, £815 10s. Stocks of materials on hand, £6,241 17s. 6d.

Jan.	1.	Bought of John Smith, 100 tons Plates at							
		£7 ..	..	..	..	..	..	£700	0 0
,,	2.	Paid him Cheque ..	..	..	..	1,200	0 0
,,	,,	Paid him Bill at 2 months	..	..	500	0 0
,,	3.	Paid Rates and Taxes	..	..	..	31	17 6

Jan.	4.	Received payment, Bill No. 248	365	0	0
,,	6.	Received Instalment, Contract No. 125..	1,000	0	0
,,	,,	Paid sundry Petty Expenses	4	16	0
,,	,,	Paid Fire Insurance	32	1	6
,,	8.	Took Contract for Anglia girders, No. 128, £1,250.			
,.	9.	Paid Bill No. 392	850	10	0
,,	,,	Bought of Peter Jones, for cash, 45 cwts. Rivets at 32s.	72	0	0
,,	,,	Material supplied to date: — Contract No. 124, £248 15s.; Contract No. 125, £132 7s. 6d.; Contract No. 127, £315 9s. 8d.; Contract No. 128, £264 7s. 6d.			
,,	11.	Received of Thomas Tiger, Cheque ..	400	0	0
,,	12.	Contract No. 126, completed and passed, and balance of contract received ..	3,500	0	0
,,	,,	Partners' Drawings : John Tough ..	500	0	0
,,	,,	Partners' Drawings : Joseph Tough ..	500	0	0
,,	13.	Bought of Henry Brown, for 2 months' bill, 50 tons Angles at £7 10s... ..	375	0	0
,,	,,	Drew Cheque for Wages this day :—Contract No. 124, £222 6s.; Contract No. 125, £107 5s.; Contract No. 126, £5 15s. 6d.; Contract No. 127, £128 18s. 6d.; Contract No. 128, £52 3s. 4d.			
,,	16.	Paid Henry Brown	430	0	0
		Discount allowed	20	0	0
,,	17.	Received of Edward Eagle	1,200	0	0
		Allowance on settlement	15	10	0
,,	18.	Received Instalment on Contract No. 124	500	0	0
,,	21.	Bought of Stephen Spicer, Timber as per invoice	142	3	6
,,	22.	Received Instalment, Contract No. 128 ..	350	0	0
,,	23.	Received Cash, Sundry Sales	18	1	6
,,	24.	Partner's Drawings, John Tough ..	150	0	0
,,	,,	Paid Peter Jones	500	0	0
,,	25.	Paid Bill No. 391, due this day	1,000	0	0
,,	,,	Received of Thomas Tiger, Bill at 3 months	841	3	6

Jan. 26.	Paid Stephen Spicer	.. .. ..	140	0	0
		Discount allowed	2	3	6
,,	27.	Drew Cheque for Wages paid this day:— Contract No. 124, £125 19s. 4d.; Contract No. 125, £22 11s.; Contract No. 127, £173 7s. 11d.; Contract No. 128, £230 4s. 4d.			
,,	,,	Received net proceeds, sale by auction of loose plant, Contract No. 126, value in books £350	186	15	0
,,	,,	Paid Office Salaries for month '.. ..	27	10	0
,,	,,	Received Instalment, Contract No. 127	1,000	0	0
,,	28.	Contract No. 125 completed and passed, Final Balance due £2,100, Instalment received	1,650	0	0
,,	29.	Paid half-year's Interest on Mortgage ..	300	0	0
,,	31.	Materials supplied to date:—Contract No. 124, £831 15s.; Contract No. 127, £463 10s.; Contract No. 128, £159 17s. 6d.			
,,	,,	Paid Water Rate	10	4	6
,,	,,	Paid Inspector's Fees, Contract No. 125	31	10	0
,,	,,	Paid off Mortgage	2,000	0	0
,,	,,	Depreciation of Buildings..	54	10	0
,,	,,	Depreciation of Plant and Machinery ..	24	6	0
,,	,,	Credit John Tough, Interest on Capital..	54	4	0
,,	,,	Credit Joseph Tough, Interest on Capital	65	15	3
,,	,,	Stock of Materials on hand	4,822	16	8